Football and Communities 2012

Series Editors

Dr Robert Fisher   Lisa Howard
Dr Ken Monteith

Advisory Board

James Arvanitakis
Katarzyna Bronk
Jo Chipperfield
Ann-Marie Cook
Peter Mario Kreuter
S Ram Vemuri

Simon Bacon
Stephen Morris
John Parry
Karl Spracklen
Peter Twohig
Kenneth Wilson

A *Research and Development* project.
http://www.inter-disciplinary.net/research/research-nexus/

Culture and Community Nexus
'Football and Communities'

In collaboration with

Manchester
Metropolitan
University

2013

Football and Communities 2012

Edited by

Deirdre Hynes and Annabel Kiernan

Inter-Disciplinary Press

Oxford, United Kingdom

The *Inter-Disciplinary Press* is part of *Inter-Disciplinary.Net* – a global network for research and publishing. The *Inter-Disciplinary Press* aims to promote and encourage the kind of work which is collaborative, innovative, imaginative, and which provides an exemplar for inter-disciplinary and multi-disciplinary publishing.

British Library Cataloguing in Publication Data. A catalogue record for this book is available from the British Library.

Inter-Disciplinary Press, Priory House, 149B Wroslyn Road, Freeland, Oxfordshire. OX29 8HR, United Kingdom.
+44 (0)1993 882087

ISBN: 978-1-84888-172-3
First published in the United Kingdom in Paperback format in 2013. First Edition.

Table of Contents

Introduction

Annabel Kiernan and Chris Porter

*****

The first annual *Football and its Communities* conference was held at Manchester Metropolitan University (MMU) on 1st June 2012. The conference was developed as part of the 2011-2012 Annual Research Programme for the Institute for Social Sciences Research (IHSSR), based in the Faculty of Humanities, Languages and Social Sciences at MMU. The theme for the wider Research Programme was 'Community' and it comprised a series of twelve events around facilitating, sustaining and engaging with our local communities.

The *Football and its Communities* conference brought together a broad and interdisciplinary research group reflecting varied points of contact with the game itself, as fans, and with wide-ranging research interests on football governance and fan engagement. The interdisciplinary emphasis was similarly reflected in the range of very engaging presentations across the conference programme as well as in the audience; a mix of academics, practitioners and fans.

The day conference, hosted in the MMU Business School, was introduced by Dr Deirdre Hynes (MMU) and the opening plenary was delivered by Professor Richard Giulianotti. In providing both a broad overview of how our understanding of football's role in society and culture has developed in recent decades, as well as deep insights into particularly relevant issues related to football and community, Professor Giulianotti initiated a suitably lively discussion amongst a very engaged and knowledgeable conference delegation. The dominant theme to emerge from this opening session was that the challenges facing football clubs, authorities, supporters and other key stakeholders – not least researchers – in contemporary society, necessitate a continuing quest for multi-disciplinary knowledge and understanding of the dynamic interplay between this uniquely popular activity and the complex, ever-changing world it operates within.

The papers (many of which are reproduced in this volume) went on to provoke vibrant discussion on themes such as equality and diversity in and at the game, nationalism(s) and shifting supporter identities, social media and technology driven transformation, the modernisation of football clubs and football fandom, the football community agenda, the politics of community football, and intention, perception and image of and within football culture. The papers reflected research expertise and football fan experience across Europe, further enriching the discussion and interaction in the panels and plenary sessions.

The evening programme, with a key theme of public engagement, was held at Manchester Town Hall and drew in further conference delegates representing football clubs, organised fans' organisations and cultural networks from Greater Manchester.

The evening session began with a short compilation of football on film, introduced by Nick Gladden from the North West Film Archive, who is the Archive's Acquisition and Documentation Officer. The audience were then addressed by Andy Pearce, project developer at the National Football Museum, who provided an introduction and 'sneak peak' of the new museum now located in Manchester which would open in July 2012. Dave Boyle, formerly Chief Executive of Supporters' Direct, then led a Q & A following his talk titled 'Football: Anything but a Business'. This provided an insightful overview of changes in fan engagement with their football clubs, the positive developments and on-going challenges around supporter ownership, and the importance of football clubs maintaining or developing genuine and meaningful relationships with their communities.

The evening was rounded off by a Panel discussion on the role of football clubs in our local communities, with a focus on community engagement and outreach working. The community development officers from clubs from across the region and from different steps of the football pyramid were represented. The panel, addressing the question: *'How has the role of football in the community changed?'* were: Andy Basterfield, Senior FIC Officer, Academy, Manchester United FC; Jonathan Elsegood, Group Sales Administrator, Bolton Wanderers FC; Gavin Makel, Football Development Manager, Manchester City FC; and Robin Pye, Community Development Officer, FC United of Manchester.

The panel discussion, chaired by Dr Steve Millington (MMU), highlighted the extensive work of all clubs in working with the communities which surround them and there was much agreement about the important role that football can play in facilitating, supporting and sustaining our communities.

With the conference representing the launch of the new Manchester Metropolitan University Football Cluster (MMUFC), we would like to thank all the participants and delegates for bringing both heat and light to our discussions of football and community and for having such a positive engagement with the event. We also thank the IHSSR for supporting our work through awarding collaborative research fellowships and providing conference funding, and Kathleen Menzies for her valuable work in editing this collection. On-going thanks also go to Dr Ann-Marie Cook and colleagues at Inter-Disciplinary.Net for publishing this volume of conference proceedings and continuing to support the continued development of our research and conference programme.

Enhancing the Match Day Experience through Technology

Philip Grundon and Darren Mundy

Abstract

Since the inception of the Premier League there has been an increasing focus on football clubs as global brands. Within this context clubs are keen to find new ways to embrace global audiences and sell their products across the world. The growth of the World Wide Web increasingly makes opportunities for global engagement with football clubs possible through websites, social media platforms, and other media forms. Fans can now increasingly interact, manipulate, and engage with materials relevant to the football club they are supporting on the match day, and outside of the match day context. However, with these changes there are increasing demands made on clubs to adapt technology to better support the fan experience. This chapter highlights developments in the entertainment sector linked to embedding interactive media based products into elements of the fan experience (e.g. programmes, stadia, and physical surroundings). Activity in this area is growing with a number of organisations (including some world renowned football clubs) starting to understand the potential of technologies such as augmented reality, touch screen interaction, mobile apps, social networking, and holographic media displays. This potential is explored in this chapter through the presentation of a number of conceptual ideas aimed at enhancing the fan experience. Finally, a discussion is presented around the impact that these new media technologies may have on fan engagement both in the context of and outside the context of the match day.

Key Words: Augmented reality, digital technologies, holographic media, match day enhancement, match day experience, social networking.

*****

1. Introduction

From the formation of the Football League in 1888,[1] fans have flocked to games to experience the unique atmosphere of the live match. For years the home of football fandom was the open terraces of football grounds,[2] but as a result of hooliganism and the horrific events of the 1989 Hillsborough Tragedy,[3] stadia were transformed into more hermeneutically sealed all-seater venues. In David Goldblatt's book,[4] *The Ball Is Round*, which documents the history of football from its roots to globalisation and its future, he notes how clubs have 'increasingly understood themselves as not just clubs, not just mere businesses, but as brands.'

This movement from clubs to brands was in part a reason for the next step in footballing history, when in 1992 satellite TV broadcaster *BSkyB* bought the TV rights for the newly formed English Premiership.[5] In the Premier league's first season it is estimated that only 8 to 10 per cent of the UK had non-terrestrial TV,[6] compare this to the 2010/2011 season, where globally 643 million homes received roughly 185,000 hours of coverage, equating to a global TV audience of 3.9 billion viewers.[7]

With the rise in satellite TV, fans have been given an alternative to the live match day experience. Mike Weed (2007) recently looked at how the pub was becoming a realistic alternative to being at the live game. He noted how the pub is very similar to the old terraced environment, with its confined atmosphere, raucous chanting, and alcohol. He describes how 'the concept of a shared communal experience' can help in 'understanding the attraction of the pub as a sport spectator venue' in addition to 'understanding the nature of the sport spectating experience' before concluding that sport spectatorship experiences should focus on the proximity 'to others sharing in the experience of watching the event' rather than the actual event itself.[8]

Liz Ellen, in her 2010 report on Increasing Attendances at Football Clubs, proposed the idea that 'clubs could improve attendances... by offering enhanced products which make the match day experience more than the basic product of the football match'.[9] After looking at different promotional schemes she expressed how they had shown innovation and ingenuity in a sport that is restricted by tradition and mentioned that modern technology would play an important part in re-engaging all categories of supporter.

It is only now that Ellen's proposal of using modern technology and Weed's concept of 'shared communal experience' are starting to be acted upon as clubs from around the globe are embracing emerging technologies and social media as a method of trying to re-engage with their fans and fan communities

This introduction provided an overview of changes in the match day experience. Section 2 will provide a detailed examination of literature related to the integration of emerging technologies in entertainment venues, football stadia and beyond. Section 3 will detail the conceptual ideas on how current and future technologies can be implemented within a stadium environment to help improve the football fans' match day experience. Finally, in Section 4 the chapter will be concluded and new directions for research detailed.

2. New Technologies and the Fan Experience

The next few sections will take an in-depth look into how clubs are utilising emerging technologies to create an enhanced experience for the fan both on the match day and away from the match day. Each section concentrates on providing specific examples of how the technology is presently being used or considered in media venues and/or fan spaces.

A. Social Media

In October 2011, the President of Barcelona F.C., Sandro Rosell explained that digital technologies would be fundamental in allowing the club to grow.[10] Didac Lee, the Director of New Technologies at Barcelona introduced a 'new digital strategy' aimed 'to generate an audience, build up brand loyalty and use that to increase ...economic resources'.[11] The clubs biggest success lies in its stunning social media presence, as of the 23rd January 2012 their Facebook page had over 25 million likes,[12] which equates to more than the population of Ghana. Recent deals with Google+ and the 'Chinese Twitter', Tencent WEIBO, have added yet more power to the Barcelona social empire.[13]

Similar to Barcelona, Manchester City have recently revamped their website to make it more fan-orientated. In 2011, Manchester City became the Premier League's first official partner of YouTube, this allowed the club to personalise their channel page, control their content rights, and manage advertising on their channel.[14] They are currently using a combination of social media and this new partnership to allow the fans to become closer to their icons. The #Ask series allowed fans to send in Twitter questions to first team players, before watching the star answer the question on the Manchester City Official YouTube channel.[15] This concept has allowed fans to discover more about the players on a social level.

This is only a taster of what Manchester City is doing in this space. In December 2011, they used the giant screens in and around their stadium to trial 'broadcasting fan's tweets from around the world' and at the game, in an attempt to make the Ethiad Stadium, a 'social media stadium',[16] and get more fans involved in topical conversations.[17]

B. Augmented Reality (AR)

At the start of the 2011/2012 season Tottenham Hotspur unveiled their new kit sponsor as Aurasma. With this sponsorship deal Spurs became the first Premier League club to utilise the 'Aurasma Experience'.[18] Aurasma is the world's first visual browser and uses advanced image and pattern recognition to recognise and understand images and objects in the real world, and then augment interactive related content known as 'Auras'.[19] Donna-Maria Cullen, Executive Director at Spurs explains the advantages of Aurasma within the football environment, 'Aurasma is an exciting technology and provides a new way to engage with our fans. It allows us to share exclusive, behind-the-scenes video content in totally new ways.' Already club merchandise such as the shirt and team photo have been Aurasma-enabled. Martina King, Managing Director of Aurasma explains that 'for the first time, traditional media such as printed newspapers can deliver the latest interactive digital content and benefit from revenue streams previously the preserve of mobile and online channels.'[20]

Manchester City are also utilising AR to engage more with their fans. In August 2011, they released their new digital membership scheme, which gave fans a RFID (Radio Frequency Identification) tagged membership card with a QR code and AR placeholder.[21] At first, Richard Ayers, head of Digital at Manchester City admitted that he did not know how to best utilise the cards potential, however, developments in December 2011, led to the announcement that fans will soon be able to use their mobile devices to access exclusive AR content, which could be shared with a friend nearby through the in-built RFID tag.[22]

C. Interactive Experiences

In 2011, Barcelona opened their new 'Camp Nou Experience' museum and tour, which incorporated an interactive multi-touch screen wall, named 'The Barca Wall of History', a multi-touch database wall and multi-touch table.[23] These multi-touch experiences combined with the actual trophies and Camp Nou tour make way for 'a unique experience that lets you feel all the emotion and thrills of Barca via the latest technology'.[24] Barcelona express how 'the renewal has seen a modern approach taken with strong technological input making the experience even better'.[25]

Clubs are not the only side of the sport to be realising the potential, stadia are trying to jump on the experience 'bandwagon'. The San Siro, home to Inter and AC Milan, recently updated their museum and tour with a new multimedia area, containing a virtual Milan derby, interactive touchscreen trivia quizzes and a digital bulletin board. The virtual Milan derby allows two or more visitors to partake in a three minute long virtual football game, whilst, the digital bulletin board allows fans to leave a digital memory to future visitors through a photo and a comment, posted to a database in the form of a digital polaroid.[26]

D. Virtual Venues and Holography

IOMEDIA and Ticketmaster's Virtual Venue solution provides a technology platform designed to enable supporters to make better or more informed choices over seat selection. This unique tool allows fans to pick any seat in a stadium and see a fully rendered 360-degree virtual view. Furthermore, fans can view their seat in different weather conditions and choose their seat on experience preferences.[27] Virtual Venue also benefits the clubs and stadium owners through its sponsorship module, which allows advertisements to be placed on the virtual versions of the big screens, TV screens and advertising hoardings.[28] Companies can also place virtual products around the venue, which also act as advertisements.[29]

In 2009, Obscura Digital unveiled the 'RockWall' a multi-touch memorabilia wall, in which visitors can interact with the many objects from multiple Hard Rock Cafés across the globe. Visitors can seamlessly swap and share objects from one end of the screen to the other, which allows for a more interactive experience.[30] In 2010, Obscura took the concept of a touchscreen to the next level through the Heineken HoloTouch experience, this holographic touchscreen allowed users to explore the brand's heritage and historic advertisements in a more interesting fashion than a normal touchscreen.[31]

In November 2011, Musion teamed up with Saatchi & Saatchi to create 'a multi-city, multi-media spectacular for the next instalment in Deutsche Telekom's "Life is for Sharing" campaign'.[32] Musion used their 3D holographic projection techniques to allow singer-songwriter Mariah Carey to perform a 20-minute Christmas concert simultaneously to five locations. The technology allowed her to interact with real dancers and the live audiences, but most impressively it allowed her to turn to fairy dust and then reform for the second song, creating a unique experience for all involved.

In 2011, Sid Lee Architects along with gsmprjct°, were challenged by Ajax Amsterdam 'to bring the passion of Ajax Football Club from the arena, back to the heart of Amsterdam'.[33] It gives fans the opportunity to experience interactive skills training areas, where visitors can hone their skills and see if they make the grade to play for Ajax. The experience takes the visitor through the heritage and history of the club, before eventually allowing them to enter a mock dressing room to receive a holographic team talk from Frank De Boer, the Ajax Manager. The culmination of the experience is to walk into a virtual recreation of the Amsterdam Arena, with audio-visual displays of fans cheering giving the visitor a sense of the live match day atmosphere in the stadium.

3. New Directions: Conceptual Ideas

The following presents original conceptual ideas linked to the technologies highlighted in Section 2.

A. External Stadium Concepts

Obscura Digital's 'Facebook Connections' (a location based visual connections application)[34] could be combined with Manchester City's RFID membership card[35] to allow fans to find or make friends at the stadium. The floor around the stadium would be interactive and as fans entered the stadium they would be logged in and instantly visual graphics on the floor would tell them if any of their known friends were already in the ground. If so it could tell them where to find them. If no friends were registered in the stadium it would point you towards other people who were by themselves with similar interests related to the club like favourite player, first season, best season, etc. Therefore allowing people who have attended alone to join in conversations and feel more part of the club's community. This technology would possibly allow foreign fans to find people who speak their language.

The San Siro's digital bulletin board[36] and Barcelona's 'Camp Nou Experience'[37] could be merged with the technology involved with Obscura Digital's 'RockWall'[38] to create a multi-touch wall that surrounds the stadium. Fans could send photos and videos with comments or tweets to a specific # tag, or they could use the screens to upload photos and comments to a continuous floating animation of photos, videos and comments, which fans could interact with in a similar way to the 'RockWall'.[39] This would allow fans from all over the world to join in with the supporters at the game. Furthermore, fans would be able to leave a memory of their experience for future visitors to read or comment on. This technology would also open up new possibilities for advertising and marketing during the week by allowing sponsors or the club to play advertisements and promotions. The screens could also be used to allow fans to buy tickets, merchandise and memorabilia.

Musion's 3D holographic projection[40] could be combined with a similar idea to Manchester City's #Ask Series[41] to create a live 3D holographic questions and answer session that would allow fans at the stadium and across the world to use social networks such as Twitter, Facebook, Google+ and Tencent WEIBO to send in questions to a player, manager or legend. Questions would be chosen at random from a live feed and would be highlighted on a screen in front of the player so they could easily answer the desired question. The player would be in a specially dedicated room with 3D holographic recording equipment, whilst the fans would be around the stadium watching and listening to the holographic representation reply to the questions from bespoke holographic pods around the ground. The holograph could also be transmitted to the club's outlets across the world [in a similar manner to how Mariah Carey performed the Christmas concert for Deutsche Telekom][42] so foreign fans could join in with the match day experience and feel closer to the club. This concept would also allow players to record skills videos in a holographic format with added graphics for in action instructions.

B. Internal Stadium Concepts

The concept of the 'Ajax Experience'[43] could be merged with the technology of the 'Camp Nou Experience'[44] to make an interactive and immersive journey through the history, philosophy and emotions of the club at the stadium. This would culminate in entering the actual stadium ready for the live match day experience. Therefore, the virtual experience would be used to enhance the pre-match build up and further increase the fans' excitement and expectations before they enter the stadium for the ultimate live fan experience.

Obscura Digital's 'HoloTouch' technology[45] could be used to allow fans to interact with the club's trophy cabinet in a virtual and interactive manner, as well as find out stats and facts about players (past and present), managers (past and present) and possibly interact with kits, memorabilia and programmes. This experience would aim to make the fan feel more immersed in the club's heritage, but in a modern and exciting way.

Aurasma (or alternative solutions) could be used to enhance the current match day programme; making it more interactive and immersive for the user. One use could be to create an interactive AR programme with videos of skills, interviews, highlights and challenges. It could also be used to create interactive quizzes and could have a page for the upload of fans' pictures which could be shown on the screens around the ground at half-time and full-time. However, perhaps the greatest benefit for the club would be the possibility to offer more immersive and interactive content to their sponsors and advertisers. Therefore such technology could be utilised to bring perimeter advertising to life, as well as, merchandise, food stalls, menus in corporate hospitality, exclusive content, and even a historic trail related to the club, which fans could take before the game.

With the combination of QR codes, RFID tags on seats and AR technology, fans would be able to leave videos, photos, comments and sound clips related to the seat and their experience. These could be stored on a chronological webpage that would allow other fans to view the seat's experience history. The aim would be to continue the process over a number of years, so that a fan in 2050 could go to the stadium [which was built in 2012] and be able to see footage of a fan's experience from the same seat on the first match day by holding their device to the seats QR code or by swiping their device across the in-built RFID tag. This concept could work like many other social networking sites with an option for people to follow certain seat histories and receive live data to their own Twitter, Facebook, Google+ and Tencent WEIBO pages.

4. Conclusion

The idea behind this study was to explore the potential of emerging technologies within the context of the fan experience. Through the research and exploration, there is an indication that football clubs are starting to embrace these technologies and recognise the potential for them to deliver increased commercial revenues. This potential extends both within the context of the match day experience and beyond. Conceptual ideas have been presented which could enhance the fan experience, however, this study also notes the current technological and financial limitations especially within the stadium environment, although clubs are investing in improving this.[46]

Future areas for exploration apart from prototypical implementation of ideas linked to the technologies described above include an analysis of business models, which emerging technologies can be used to exploit, the notion of experience, and how technologies such as those identified can impact upon the fan experience, and understanding how new technological infrastructures within stadia can be used to deliver enhanced experiences. Ultimately the concept of capturing a sense of media histories within performance stadia (e.g. capturing the sense of the moment) should be the focus for any future research into this area.

Notes

[1] Ivor Baddiel, *Ultimate Football* (Revised ed. London: Dorling Kindersley Ltd., 2000), 9.

[2] Hugh Hornby, *Dorling Kindersley Eyewitness Guides: Football* (London: Dorling Kindersley Ltd, 2000), 47.

[3] Ian Cruise, 'Fan Culture,' in *The Concise Encyclopedia of World Football: Updated Edition*, ed. Glenn Moore (Bath: Parragon, 2001), 180-183.

[4] David Goldblatt, *The Ball is Round: A Global History of Football* (London: Penguin Books Ltd, 2007), 683.

[5] Ibid.

[6] Mike Weed, 'The Pub as a Virtual Football Fandom Venue: An Alternative to "Being There"?' *Soccer & Society* 8.2-3 (2007): 408.

[7] Barclays Premier League, *Research & Insight 2010/2011* (London, Barclays Premier League, 2011). http://fansurvey.premierleague.com/.

[8] Mike Weed, 'The Pub,' 411.

[9] Liz Ellen, *Increasing Attendances at Football Clubs* (London: Mischon de Reya, 2010), 9. http://www.mishcon.com/assets/managed/docs/downloads/doc_2420/Increasing_A ttendances_in_the_Football_League_-_March_2010.pdf.

[10] Vanessa Forns, 'Club: FC Barcelona makes firm commitment to new technologies,' last accessed January 2012. http://www.fcbarcelona.com/club/detail/article/fc-barcelona-makes-firm-commit ment-to-new-technologies.

[11] Ibid.

[12] FC Barcelona, 'Official FC Barcelona Facebook Page,' last accessed January 2012, http://www.facebook.com/fcbarcelona?sk=app_11007063052.

[13] FC Barcelona, 'Club: Sandro Rosell Sees New Technology in Asia as "The Only Way to Increase Income",' last accessed January 2012, http://www.fcbarcelona.com/club/detail/article/sandro-rosell-sees-new-technology-in-asia-as-the-only-way-to-increase-income.

[14] Football Marketing.com, 'Manchester City Strikes Content Deal with YouTube,' last accessed January 2012, http://www.football-marketing.com/2011/10/12/manchester-city-youtube-deal/.

[15] Manchester City, 'Manchester City's Official YouTube Channel,' last accessed January 2012, http://www.youtube.com/user/mcfcofficial.

[16] Sean Walsh, 'Manchester City Take a Step Closer to the "Social Media Stadium",' Last accessed January 2012, http://digital-football.com/sports-social-media/2011/12/02/manchester-city-take-a-step-closer-to-the-social-media-stadium/.

[17] Paul, Sawers, 'Manchester City Football Club to Broadcast Fans' Tweets on Giant Screens,' *The Next Web.com* (blog), December 2nd 2011, http://thenextweb.com/uk/2011/12/02/manchester-city-football-club-to-broadcast-fans-tweets-on-giant-screens/.

[18] Tottenham Hotspur, 'Tottenham Hotspur Unveil World's First Ever Aurasma-Enabled Team Shirt,' last accessed January 2012,
http://www.tottenhamhotspur.com/news/articles/tottenham-hotspur-unveil-aurasma
-enabled-shirt-011011.html.

[19] Business Weekly, 'Tech City Uses Aurasma Cambridge App,' *Business Weekly*, November 11, 2011, http://www.businessweekly.co.uk/hi-tech/13068-tech-city-uses-aurasma-cambridge-app.

[20] Aurasma, 'Aurasma and United Daily News Partner to Create World's First Augmented National Newspaper,' last accessed January 2012,
http://www.aurasma.com/news.jsp.

[21] Robert Andrews, 'Interview: The World's Richest Soccer Club Is Like A Free Content "Startup".' *paidContent:UK*,
http://paidcontent.co.uk/article/419-the-worlds-richest-soccer-club-is-like-a-free-content-startup/.

[22] Michael Barnett, and Lara O'Reilly, 'Man City to Extend Members Scheme to Include Swappable Content,' *Marketing Week*, December 15, 2011,
http://www.marketingweek.co.uk/sectors/sport/man-city-to-extend-members-scheme-to-include-swappable-content/3032752.article.

[23] FC Barcelona, 'Camp Nou: Changing Times,' last accessed January 2012,
http://www.fcbarcelona.com/camp-nou/museum/detail/card/changing-times;
FC Barcelona, 'Camp Nou: Multimedia area,' Last accessed January 2012,
http://www.fcbarcelona.com/camp-nou/camp-nou-experience/detail/card/
multimedia-area.

[24] Ibid.

[25] FC Barcelona, 'Camp Nou: Restructuring Programme,' Last accessed January 2012,
http://www.fcbarcelona.com/camp-nou/museum/detail/card/restructuring-programme.

[26] San Siro Museum & Tour, 'New Multimedia Hall: Virtual Experience,' Last accessed January 2012, http://www.sansirotour.com/saladegasperi-ing.htm.

[27] IOMEDIA, 'Demonstration Video,' Last accessed January 2012,
http://www.io-virtualvenue.com/demonstration-video/index.html.

[28] IOMEDIA, 'Virtual Venue: Features & Benefits,' last accessed January 2012,
http://www.io-virtualvenue.com/features/index.html.

[29] IOMEDIA, 'Demonstration Video.'

[30] Obscura Digital, 'Rock Wall: Hard Rock Café Multitouch Memorabilia Wall,' Last accessed January 2012,
http://www.obscuradigital.com/work/detail/rock-wall/.

[31] Obscura Digital, 'Heineken HoloTouch: Holographic Touchscreen Display,' Last accessed January 2012, http://www.obscuradigital.com/work/detail/heineken-holotouch2/.

[32] Isobel Kerr-Newell., 'Holographic World First from Deutsche Telekom and Saatchi & Saatchi,' Last accessed January 2012, http://www.saatchi.com/news/archive/holographic_world_first_from_deutsche_tel ekom_and_saatchi__saatchi.

[33] Sidleetv, 'Sid Lee Architecture: The Ajax Experience,' last accessed January 2012, http://www.youtube.com/watch?v=sacqRFwgsYI.

[34] Obscura Digital, 'Connections for Facebook: Mapping Physical Social Graph Data,' last accessed January 2012, http://www.obscuradigital.com/work/detail/f8/.

[35] Michael Barnett, and Lara O'Reilly, 'Man City.'

[36] San Siro Museum & Tour, 'Multimedia Hall.'

[37] FC Barcelona, 'Changing Times.'

[38] Obscura Digital, 'Rock Wall.'

[39] Ibid.

[40] Musion, 'Musion Website,' last accessed January 2012, http://www.musion.co.uk/index.html.

[41] Manchester City, 'YouTube'.

[42] Isobel Kerr-Newell., 'Holographic World.'

[43] Sidleetv, 'Ajax Experience'.

[44] FC Barcelona, 'Changing Times.'

[45] Obscura Digital, 'Touchscreen Display.'

[46] Vanessa Forns, 'New Technologies.'; Real Madrid, 'Real Madrid and Cisco Sign Agreement to Turn Bernabeu into Most Technologically Advanced Stadium in Europe,' last accessed January 2012, http://www.realmadrid.com/cs/Satellite/en/1330072431891/noticia/Noticia/Real_ Madrid_and_Cisco_sign_agreement_to_turn_Bernabeu_into_most_technologically _advanced_stadium.htm.

Bibliography

Andrews, Robert. 'Interview: The World's Richest Soccer Club Is Like A Free Content "Startup".' *paidContent:UK*. http://paidcontent.co.uk/article/419-the-worlds-richest-soccer-club-is-like-a-free-content-startup/.

Aurasma, 'Aurasma and United Daily News Partner to Create World's First Augmented National Newspaper.' Last accessed January 2012. http://www.aurasma.com/news.jsp.

Baddiel, Ivor. *Ultimate Football*. Revised ed. London: Dorling Kindersley Ltd., 2000.

Barclays Premier League. *Research & Insight 2010/2011*. London, Barclays Premier League, 2011. http://fansurvey.premierleague.com/.

Barnett, Michael and Lara O'Reilly. 'Man City to Extend Members Scheme to Include Swappable Content.' *Marketing Week*. December 15, 2011. http://www.marketingweek.co.uk/sectors/sport/man-city-to-extend-members-scheme-to-include-swappable-content/3032752.article.

Business Weekly. 'Tech City Uses Aurasma Cambridge App.' *Business Weekly*. November 11, 2011. http://www.businessweekly.co.uk/hi-tech/13068-tech-city-uses-aurasma-cambridge-app.

Cruise, Ian. 'Fan Culture.' In *The Concise Encyclopedia of World Football: Updated Edition*, edited by Glenn Moore, 180-183. Bath: Parragon, 2001.

Ellen, Liz. *Increasing Attendances at Football Clubs*. London: Mischon de Reya, 2010. http://www.mishcon.com/assets/managed/docs/downloads/doc_2420/Increasing_Attendances_in_the_Football_League_-_March_2010.pdf.

FC Barcelona, 'Camp Nou: Changing Times.' Last accessed January 2012. http://www.fcbarcelona.com/camp-nou/museum/detail/card/changing-times.

FC Barcelona, 'Camp Nou: Multimedia Area.' Last accessed January 2012. http://www.fcbarcelona.com/camp-nou/camp-nou-experience/detail/card/multimedia-area.

FC Barcelona, 'Official FC Barcelona Facebook Page.' Last accessed January 2012, http://www.facebook.com/fcbarcelona?sk=app_11007063052.

FC Barcelona, 'Camp Nou: Restructuring Programme.' Last accessed January 2012. http://www.fcbarcelona.com/camp-nou/museum/detail/card/restructuring-programme.

FC Barcelona, 'Club: Sandro Rosell Sees New Technology in Asia as "The only Way to Increase Income".' Last accessed January 2012. http://www.fcbarcelona.com/club/detail/article/sandro-rosell-sees-new-technology-in-asia-as-the-only-way-to-increase-income.

Forns, Vanessa. 'Club: FC Barcelona Makes Firm Commitment to New Technologies.' Last accessed January 2012.
http://www.fcbarcelona.com/club/detail/article/fc-barcelona-makes-firm-commitment-to-new-technologies.

Football Marketing.com, 'Manchester City Strikes Content Deal with YouTube.' Last accessed January 2012.
http://www.football-marketing.com/2011/10/12/manchester-city-youtube-deal/.

Goldblatt, David. *The Ball is Round: A Global History of Football*. London: Penguin. Books Ltd, 2007.

Hornby, Hugh. *Dorling Kindersley Eyewitness Guides: Football*. London: Dorling Kindersley Ltd, 2000.

IOMEDIA, 'Demonstration Video.' Last accessed January 2012.
http://www.io-virtualvenue.com/demonstration-video/index.html.

IOMEDIA, 'Virtual Venue: Features & Benefits.' Last accessed January 2012.
http://www.io-virtualvenue.com/features/index.html.

Kerr-Newell, Isobel. 'Holographic World First from Deutsche Telekom and Saatchi & Saatchi.' Last accessed January 2012.
http://www.saatchi.com/news/archive/holographic_world_first_from_deutsche_telekom_and_saatchi__saatchi.

Manchester City, 'Manchester City's Official YouTube Channel.' Last accessed January 2012. http://www.youtube.com/user/mcfcofficial.

Musion, 'Musion Website.' Last accessed January 2012.
http://www.musion.co.uk/index.html.

Obscura Digital, 'Connections for Facebook: Mapping Physical Social Graph Data.' Last accessed January 2012. http://www.obscuradigital.com/work/detail/f8/.

Obscura Digital, 'Heineken HoloTouch: Holographic Touchscreen Display.' Last accessed January 2012.
http://www.obscuradigital.com/work/detail/heineken-holotouch2/.

Obscura Digital, 'Rock Wall: Hard Rock Café Multitouch Memorabilia Wall.' Last accessed January 2012. http://www.obscuradigital.com/work/detail/rock-wall/.

Real Madrid, 'Real Madrid and Cisco Sign Agreement to Turn Bernabeu into Most Technologically Advanced Stadium in Europe.' Last accessed January 2012. http://www.realmadrid.com/cs/Satellite/en/1330072431891/noticia/Noticia/Real.

San Siro Museum & Tour, 'New Multimedia Hall: Virtual Experience.' Last accessed January 2012. http://www.sansirotour.com/saladegasperi-ing.htm.

Sawers, Paul. 'Manchester City Football Club to Broadcast Fans' Tweets on Giant Screens.' The Next Web.com. http://thenextweb.com/uk/2011/12/02/manchester-city-football-club-to-broadcast-fans-tweets-on-giant-screens/.

Sidleetv, 'Sid Lee Architecture: The Ajax Experience.' Last accessed January 2012. http://www.youtube.com/watch?v=sacqRFwgsYI.

Tottenham Hotspur, 'Tottenham Hotspur Unveil World's First Ever Aurasma-Enabled Team Shirt.' Last accessed January 2012. http://www.tottenhamhotspur.com/news/articles/tottenham-hotspur-unveil-aurasma-enabled-shirt-011011.html.

Walsh, Sean. 'Manchester City Takes a Step Closer to the "Social Media Stadium".' Last accessed January 2012. http://digital-football.com/sports-social-media/2011/12/02/manchester-city-take-a-step-closer-to-the-social-media-stadium/.

Weed, Mike. 'The Pub as a Virtual Football Fandom Venue: An Alternative to "Being there"?' Soccer & Society 8.2-3 (2007): 399-414.

Can Football Journalists Satisfy the Demands of their Communities in an Age of Citizen Journalism and Social Media?

Paul Clark

Abstract

Since the Victorian era, the mainstay of local newspapers has been the sports section. In footballing heartlands such as Manchester, Liverpool and Glasgow this part of the chapter, though seemingly side-lined to the back pages, has often been its lifeblood. Sports journalists have turned out copy to satisfy the readers' demands even on days when new information was hard to come by. Football has changed, so too has the appetite of this readership; they are no longer just interested in the usual transfer speculation and match reports but given the business aspects of the game have become as equally concerned with these issues too. As the football business has increased, the coverage of financial matters has not always been forthcoming in some newspapers but has been left to bloggers and social media enthusiasts to uncover. This has been evidenced by The Rangers Tax Case blog, which has dealt with the issues at Glasgow Rangers and highlighted how they stole a march on the mainstream journalists in exposing the issues at the club. This chapter will look at the function of blogs and social media taking on the role of the fourth estate in highlighting issues occasionally neglected by the press. The regional press and to a certain extent the nationals have a difficult relationship with football clubs in terms of being granted access. In some quarters this relationship is portrayed as subservient and acquiescent to the clubs in trade for access. Furthermore the chapter will discuss the difficulties football journalists have in their relationships with clubs as a possible factor in the reasons why some information is not published by mainstream publications and is left to single-issue social media enthusiasts to uncover.

Key Words: Blogging, citizen journalism, fanzines, football journalism, online journalism, sports journalism.

*****

Today there is a wealth of football journalism; content has increased as the traditional journalism model has changed. This coverage has moved beyond the limitations of the back pages and now embraces match reports and transfer gossip, as well as content related to the business aspects of the game.

These changes have also democratised the landscape for non-mainstream writers to become their own media. With it the readership/community relationship has changed – they have gone from being passive receivers of information with a modicum of input, to being able to comment using the various platforms available.

Given the age we are in, this has raised the question as to whether or not traditional media now serves the needs of particular football communities.

This chapter will look at these developments and will look at the challenges faced by football journalists today. The community that this chapter will deal with is that covered mainly by local/regional media, though for the issues pertaining to Glasgow Rangers, that definition of the local has something of a national dimension too.

The emergence of the amateur journalist, or the citizen journalist, has its origins in the fanzine movement. The fanzine has been considered from within cultural studies or cultural sociology, as a 'site for cultural contestation.'[1] This form characterised a number of publications from the 1980s, which originated out of dissent, with supporters opposing the introduction of ID Cards or the general running of the game. Fanzines often played a role in the cultural politics of a club too, in some cases these publications defined a club's culture, taking a stance against things such as racism, sexism, hooliganism, commercialisation and policing – the Manchester United fanzine *Red Action* and the fanzine of Hibernian, called *The Proclaimer* – were both inspired by their founders' desire to challenge racist chants among their fellow supporters.[2] One of the first football fanzines, *Foul*, ran between 1972 and 1976. One of its writers, Chris Lightbown, created the publication because 'football had simply not assimilated any of the social or cultural changes of the sixties. It was in a complete time warp.'[3]

As technology has developed the print publications have been replaced with online formats, a number of football publications were first to embrace the online medium and have increasingly become a voice for marginalised fans, Liverpool and Manchester United supporters used them as a forum to discuss the perceived failings of their respective American owners. 'Fomented by internet forums and talk radio, the unrest at England's richest and most successful football club appeared on both the front and back pages of newspapers.'[4] In Liverpool, the Spirit of Shankly group, used all the means available to them oust their unpopular owners via social networking, by using Twitter their campaign gained more support and awareness in the media.

Manchester United fans set up 'Shareholders against Murdoch' in protest against the takeover by the newspaper magnate; this organisation became Manchester United Supporters Trust (MUST) and they have continued to protest against the Glazer Family's ownership of the club. Blogs such as *Andersred* have delved a little deeper into the finances, sometimes when mainstream media have ignored the finer detail. The blog, written by Andy Green, a fund manager and fan sympathetic to MUST, forensically details the extent of the club's financial situation with great detail, so much so, that whenever stories about United's finances appear in the mainstream press Andersred is invariably quoted.

In some cases when the mainstream media has neglected certain issues bloggers and citizen journalists have plugged the gaps. The media in Scotland has received criticism for its coverage of the financial plight of Glasgow Rangers FC, (which was liquidated in the summer of 2012) – a club described by Scottish Journalist Graham Spiers as 'one of the three great pillars of society (alongside the church and the law in Scotland).'[5] Their troubles had been on-going for a number of years but reached critical levels in February 2012, when the club entered into administration. The accusation against the media has been one of complicity and standing by watching the club lurch from crisis to crisis.

The Rangers Tax Case blog, started, according to its anonymous author, 'as an impulse one Sunday in March 2011.'[6] This online publication has charted the financial issues that have beset Rangers, to a greater depth than that of the mainstream media in Scotland over a longer period. Given the delicate nature of the particular tensions in Scottish football, the blog is written under the cloak of anonymity, which is something that the blogger discounts as a problem 'with mindless tribalism masquerading as a religious divide, stabbings, live bombs sent through the post, and even murders have been woven into the tapestry of the recent history of Scottish football. Yet I still get challenged over my penchant for anonymity?'[7]

What has been written anonymously should not be discounted, as some of the best investigative journalism has been produced anonymously. In the best journalistic traditions the sources have remained anonymous but there have been clues to where the sources may be coming from 'anyone reading the blog again would see that my sources of information probably lie outside of the government.'[8] The credibility of the blog is further enhanced by the fact that the content has gone beyond half-baked 'I know a secret'[9] origins to become a forum for citizen journalism. The nature of the pressures faced by bloggers and mainstream media alike in such a hotbed as Glasgow, can be highlighted by the intimations and threats to the SFA panel that placed a transfer embargo on the club, 'the three man panel has been the subject of vile abuse over Twitter (that old chestnut) for objectively making a decision based on the facts laid out in front of them.'[10] The success of the blog can be seen with its daily traffic of over 100,000 views[11] – by the end of May 2012 it was receiving 122,084 daily views, even on days when it didn't publish a new blog post.[12] The blog has even been the recipient of an Orwell Award and was described as 'a worthy winner which not only proves that independent blogging is as healthy as it ever was, but also offers a mirror in which our times are reflected.'[13]

As well as highlighting the issues at the club, the blog sees its purpose as holding to account the media in Scotland and their perceived complicity in the club's predicament. In the eyes of the blogger these failings have been detrimental to the club's supporters, 'Ultimately it was the supporters who were not well served by this course of action as [the fans] were deceived by a media pack that had to know that the stories it peddled were false.'[14]

The theme of complicity that the blog has highlighted has been taken on by other parts of the media, Alex Thompson *Channel 4 News* chief correspondent has claimed, 'for years too much football "journalism" in Glasgow had been too lazy, sycophantic and incapable of asking awkward questions,'[15] he likened the coverage to that of the bankers. This accusation was not well received by the journalists he questioned:

> Sarajevo, Mogadishu, Kabul, Islamabad, Tripoli, Baghdad ... I could bore you with more – in none of these places have I ever got this interesting reaction from local journalists. Only in Glasgow. So something's up. Something's different. Something about asking questions about RFC clearly angers some in the Glasgow media in a way I've never seen in 25 years of global reporting.[16]

In a similar timescale to the Rangers crisis, a number of Everton fan groups had concerns, about the ownership of their club. They similarly accused the local media of complicity with the owner of the club. Though the issues facing Everton are not on the scale of Rangers, there were still concerns about the lack of investment. The fan groups claimed that the picture painted by the media was that Everton were a well-run club and not imperilled like other high profile Premier League clubs.

Mainly because of its proximity, the *Liverpool Echo* bore the brunt of the fans frustrations (though national media organisations were targeted by the campaign). In an open letter in December 2011 to the *Liverpool Echo*'s sports editor John Thompson, they claimed by publishing the letter on their website it was 'as proof to Everton supporters that The People's Group are lobbying the local media for more coverage of the affairs inside the corridors of Goodison Park'. The letter added: 'We would hope the *Liverpool Echo* (the self-styled "The Voice of Merseyside") listens to its people and indeed has read our correspondence even if they do not see fit to reply to us.'[17] The letter ran to over 3,500 words and was well considered and included links to the appropriate evidence of the points that they were trying to highlight. Though there were some barbed comments in the letter that may have seemed provocative to certain aspects of the local media. 'We are aware that certain media outlets are close to the club, or even "friendly" with certain board members, so we will be monitoring how this gets reported.'[18]

The scrutiny for sports journalists at times can be intense – in years gone by this would have been via the letter sent in green ink and capital letters. Today with much of the content being posted online – there is an almost automated chance to interact with what has been written. With journalists using social networking sites such as Twitter, the scrutiny has intensified as Mark Segal notes:

> Before social media created a two-way conversation on the internet, a journalist would only have had their editor and

probably the manager of the club they reported on to answer to. They could print stories knowing they would not be asked to justify them to the ordinary football fan. But it's different now for those who have chosen to set up Twitter accounts. They are pulled up on any factual errors in their stories, asked to reveal their sources and generally badgered by their followers.[19]

This chapter has dealt with the criticisms of the perceived failings of sports journalism, it is important to address factors why this may be. The role needs to be understood in context. Football and sports journalists have faced criticism in the past about what they do as being akin to that of the 'toy department', where the less serious journalism takes place. Today they are also expected to also fulfil the watchdog responsibilities that have long been associated with news journalists, as well as be experts in their field. 'Sports journalists are expected, often at the same time, to be objective reporters, critical investigators apologists for sports and teams, representatives of fans, and not unusually, to have performed in sport at the elite levels.'[20] There are investigative sports journalists out there such as Andrew Jennings and David Conn but because this type of journalism is considered to be something of a rarity, this is seen as a negative for the profession. The role also needs to be understood against the backdrop of unprecedented change that is taking place in the media. Though there is a level of expectancy, especially in cities such as Liverpool and Glasgow that journalists are in tune with this fervour they expect to have their prejudices reflected by the local media.[21] This relationship can be highlighted by Rob Steen's quote, in a chapter entitled 'The Hardest Job I Ever Craved' he states that:

> Balancing objective reporting with local loyalty, the expectations of your readers and editor, and the need to maintain a working relationship with clubs and officials with whom you may have daily contact, is as difficult as journalism gets. The rump of sportswriters are employed by local and regional titles, moreover, and hence walk such a tightrope every day. All the more reason to use temperate language and resist rushing to judgement.[22]

The, publish and be damned nature of blogs is a world away from role of a regional journalist. As Steen's quote highlights the proximity of a reporter sees them having to temper their reporting so that what they write is not overly critical. Contacts and links with a club are the lifeblood of a journalist – without this access the reporter would not be privy to a manager's thoughts and unable to get the exclusives that their editor and readership demands.

Being too close as was suggested by the Blue Union letter, as well as in numerous posts on the Rangers Tax Blog,

> The Irish Times sportswriter Tom Humphries has identified the
> danger for journalists of "travelling too close to the circus" or the
> intrinsic complicity of sports journalism with its over reliance
> access to sources among elite sports organisations and
> individuals.[23]

The perceived complicity was highlighted by the blog when they suggested that Rangers supply of transfer 'exclusives' and player trivia to ensure that the hack does not have to work hard. Any Scottish journalist wishing to have a long career learns quickly not to 'bite the hands that feed'.[24] Graham Spiers from his time at the *Glasgow Herald* highlighted many of the issues facing the beat reporter in a city such as Glasgow,

> The Herald wants me to interview Alex McLeish [then manager
> of Rangers], but they also want me to be very robust editorially
> about Rangers. You then try to get an interview and Rangers say
> no because of the coverage in your paper.[25]

In big cities such as Manchester, Liverpool and Glasgow there is always a need for the slightest morsel of information about each of the clubs, even on the slowest of news days. This is a commercial imperative more than anything, it is important that there is a steady stream of stories involving the big football teams which is absolutely vital for the commercial success of papers in these cities.[26]

When mainstream journalists do ask telling questions at press conferences they face the prospect by being 'left outside the tent'. As Associated Press sports reporter Rob Harris found out when he asked a question about Ryan Giggs at a press conference 'how important?' the Welshman would be for Saturday's Champions League final against Barcelona,[27] following a week of intense speculation about his private life. Sir Alex Ferguson was caught on *Sky TV* asking who the reporter was and could he be banned for the press conference later in the week.

When the *Liverpool Echo* did finally question what was going on at Everton, they were seemingly subjected to a ban 'that denied access to players and staff as well as press-conferences, they then had to make do with reporting second-hand news and by writing filler comment-pieces.'[28] This was after the publication of a series of features, which the club declined to participate in, by the paper's political correspondent entitled 'Just what does the future hold for the Blues?' This scrutiny was seemingly the catalyst for the paper to receive a ban.

One newspaper that has 'bitten the hand' was *The Lancashire Evening Telegraph* they realised that their local club was out of step with the community.

The Lancashire Evening Telegraph used a front page to post an editorial about the incumbent Blackburn Rovers manager Steve Keen. Given the fervour of negative feeling towards the club at the time they took the step to print a front page editorial.[29] This was a calculated step by the paper knowing that the club's regime was so poorly thought of, that they would not try to ban the local newspaper given the height of the anger felt by the supporters.

In response to the question posed at the outset, football journalists these days probably cannot satisfy the demands of their communities. As fan groups/ communities can never really be satisfied with the coverage that they are getting. That is why they have taken to social media to get their side of the story out into the public domain. This is not to say that the football journalists do not strive to do so but with the increase in attention they receive it becomes more difficult by the day. The plurality of information can be a good thing but for the sports journalist it can also be a bad thing. Given the issues that are facing mainstream journalists the pressures to get the story are still there but also not to 'bite the hand that feeds' also the wealth of information available should strike a note of caution to the journalist too. 'The current media environment has also created other problems for sports writers. Not only do sports writers have to compete with bloggers but they also are often forced to spend hours tracking down false leads that appeared on the internet.'[30]

The accusations of complicity are difficult to justify given the way that clubs some football operate these days, the mere hint of straying from the line then the clubs deny all access.

Notes

[1] Jary et al. 1991, cited in Chris Atton, *Current Issues in Alternative Media Research* (School of Creative Industries, Napier University Sociology Compass, 2007), 282.

[2] Raymond Boyle, *Sports Journalism: Context and Issues* (Thousand Oaks: Sage Publications, 2006).

[3] Andy Lyons and Barney Ronay, *When Saturday Comes: The Half Decent Football Book* (London, New York: Penguin Books, 2005), 138.

[4] Sam Knight, 'Football's New Age of Fan Power?' Last modified 24 August 2010, accessed 17 May 2012,
http://www.prospectmagazine.co.uk/2010/08/footballs-new-age-of-fan-power.

[5] Graham Spiers, 'Ecstasy and Agony of Rangers Fans,' last modified 15 February 2012, accessed 17 May 2012,
http://www.scotsman.com/the-scotsman/opinion/comment/graham-spiers-ecstasy-and-agony-for-rangers-fans-1-2119018.

[6] Ranger's Tax Case, 'My Blog Shows How Scotland's Media were Complicit in Rangers' Fall,' last modified 17 February 2012, accessed 17 May 2012, http://www.guardian.co.uk/football/blog/2012/feb/17/scotland-media-rangers.

[7] Ibid.

[8] Ibid.

[9] Ibid.

[10] Chris Nuttall, 'Has Fan Power Gone Too Far?' Last modified 30 May 2012, accessed 30 May 2012, http://www.footballeditorial.com/2012/04/opinion-has-fan-power-gone-too-far.

[11] Rangers Tax Case, 'My Blog Shows.'

[12] @rangerstaxcase, 30 May 2012, comment on *Rangers Tax-Case* Twitter account, https://twitter.com/rangerstaxcase/status/207746699517628416.

[13] Sam Jones, 'Guardian Journalist Amelia Gentleman Wins Orwell Prize,' last modified 2 May 2012, accessed 17 May 2012, http://www.guardian.co.uk/media/2012/may/24/guardian-amelia-gentleman-orwell -prize?newsfeed=true.

[14] Rangers Tax Case, 'My Blog Shows.'

[15] Alex Thompson, 'Rangers: How Come Nobody Saw This Coming?' last modified 5 April 2011, accessed 17 May 2012, http://blogs.channel4.com/alex-thomsons-view/rangers-coming/1088.

[16] Hamish Mackay, 'Alex Thomson Threatened over "lazy journalism" Jibe,' last modified 1 April 2011, accessed 17 May 2012, http://www.pressgazette.co.uk/story.asp?sectioncode=1&storycode=49093&c=1.

[17] The Blue Union, 'Our Letter,' last modified 11 December 2011, accessed 17 May 2012, http://www.theblueunion.com/news/peoples-group-letter-to-the-echo.

[18] The People's Group, 'The People's Group Letter to the Liverpool Echo Sports Editor,' last modified 9 December 2011, accessed 17 May 2012, http://peoplesgroup.wordpress.com/2011/12/09/the-peoples-group-letter-to-the-liverpool-echo-sports-editor.

[19] Mark Segal, 'A Tending Topic,' last modified 7 June 2011, accessed 17 May 2012, http://www.wsc.co.uk/content/view/5434/38.

[20] Raymond Boyle, *Sports Journalism: Context and Issues* (Thousand Oaks, CA: Sage Publications, 2006), 15.

[21] Phil Andrews, *Sports Journalism: A Practical Guide* (Thousand Oaks, CA: Sage Publications, 2005).

[22] Rob Steen, *Sports Journalism: A Multimedia Primer* (Abingdon, Oxon: Taylor & Francis Ltd., 2008), 17.

[23] Raymond Boyle, *Sports Journalism*, 118.

[24] Rangers Tax Case, 'My Blog Shows.'

[25] Raymond Boyle, *Sports Journalism*, 96.

[26] Ibid., 47.

[27] Paul Linford, 'Press Gazette Editor Hits out at "Pathetic" Fergie over Bid to Ban Journalist,' last modified 25 May 2011, accessed 17 May 2012. http://www.holdthefrontpage.co.uk/2011/news/editor-hits-out-at-pathetic-fergie-over-bid-to-ban-journalist.

[28] 'Everton FC: You're Banned,' *Other Tall Stories*, last modified March 15, 2011, accessed 17 May 2012, http://othertallstories.wordpress.com/2011/03/15/everton-fc-youre-banned.

[29] Telegraph Editorial, 'Lancashire Telegraph Comment: Time to Go Steve Kean,' last modified 19 December 2011, accessed 17 May 2012, http://www.lancashiretelegraph.co.uk/sport/9427073.Lancashire_Telegraph_comment__Time_to_go_Steve.

[30] Scott Reinardy and Wayne Wanta, *The Essentials of Sports Reporting* (London: Routledge, 2009), 7.

Bibliography

Andrews, Phil. *Sports Journalism: A Practical Guide*. Sage Publications, 2005.

Atton, Chris. *Current Issues in Alternative Media Research*. School of Creative Industries, Napier University Sociology Compass, 2007.

Bartlett, David. 'Everton FC in Focus: Just what does the Future Hold for the Blues?' Last modified 15 February 2012. http://www.liverpoolecho.co.uk/liverpool-news/local-news/2011/02/15/everton-fc-in-focus-just-what-does-the-future-hold-for-the-blues-100252-28171353/#ixzz1wNPUVwGx.

The Blue Union. 'Our Letter.' Last modified 11 December 2011. http://www.theblueunion.com/news/peoples-group-letter-to-the-echo.

Boyle, Raymond. *Sports Journalism: Context and Issues*. Sage Publications, 2006.

Cleland, Jamie. 'The Media and Football Supporters: A Changing Relationship.' *Media Culture Society* 33, Issue 2 (Sage Publications, 2009): 299-315.

Davies, Christopher. 'Club Ban Paper…So Paper Ban Club.' Last modified 10 April 2012. http://www.footballwriters.co.uk/editorial/club-ban-paper-so-paper-ban-club.

Green, Andy. 'The Scale of Fenway's Challenge at Liverpool becomes Clear.' Last modified 4 May 2012. http://andersred.blogspot.co.uk/2012/05/scale-of-fenways-challenge-at-liverpool.html.

Hepburn, Iain. 'One more Time: Roses for Rangers Tax Blog and Raspberries for Roy Greenslade.' Last modified 30 December 30 2011. http://www.thedrum.co.uk/opinion/2011/12/30/one-more-time.

Hurrell, Stephen. 'Opinion: "In The Know"? Stop the Lies, Twitter.' Last modified 29 May 2012. http://www.footballeditorial.com/2012/05/opinion-in-the-know-stop-the-lies-twitter.

Jones, Sam. 'Guardian Journalist Amelia Gentleman Wins Orwell Prize.' Last modified 2 May 2012. http://www.guardian.co.uk/media/2012/may/24/guardian-amelia-gentleman-orwell-prize?newsfeed=true.

Knight, Sam. 'Football's New Age of Fan Power?' Last modified August 24, 2010. http://www.prospectmagazine.co.uk/2010/08/footballs-new-age-of-fan-power.

Linford, Paul. 'Press Gazette Editor Hits out at "Pathetic" Fergie over Bid to Ban Journalist.' Last modified 25 May 2011. http://www.holdthefrontpage.co.uk/2011/news/editor-hits-out-at-pathetic-fergie-over-bid-to-ban-journalist.

Lyons, Andy, and Barney Ronay. *When Saturday Comes: The Half Decent Football Book.* Penguin Books. 2005

Mackay, Hamish. 'Alex Thomson Threatened over "Lazy Journalism" Jibe.' Last modified 1 April 2011. http://www.pressgazette.co.uk/story.asp?sectioncode=1&storycode=49093&c=1.

McConville, Paul. 'Can Blogs Like Rangers Tax Case Take Over from Mainstream Media?' Last modified 4 December 2011. http://scotslawthoughts.wordpress.com/2011/12/04/can-blogs-like-rangers-tax-case-take-over-from-mainstream-media.

Nuttall, Chris. 'Has Fan Power Gone Too Far?' Last modified 30 May 2012. http://www.footballeditorial.com/2012/04/opinion-has-fan-power-gone-too-far.

Other Tall Stories. 'Everton FC: You're Banned.' Last modified 15 March 2011. http://othertallstories.wordpress.com/2011/03/15/everton-fc-youre-banned.

The People's Group. 'The People's Group Letter to the Liverpool Echo Sports Editor.' Last modified 9 December 2011. http://peoplesgroup.wordpress.com/2011/12/09/the-peoples-group-letter-to-the-liverpool-echo-sports-edit.

Rangers Tax Case. 'A Victim of our Own Success.' 6 February 2012. http://rangerstaxcase.wordpress.com/2012/02/06/a-victim-of-our-own-success.

Rangers Tax Case. 'Blogger Scoops Mainstream Media yet again, Shocker!: In Spare Time.' Last modified 14 February 2012. http://rangerstaxcase.wordpress.com/2012/02/14/amateur-humiliates-mainstream-media.

Rangers Tax Case. Comment on *Rangers Tax-Case* Twitter account. 30 May 2012. https://twitter.com/rangerstaxcase/status/207746699517628416.

Rangers Tax Case. 'Ibrox Confidential.' Last modified 7 February 2012. http://rangerstaxcase.wordpress.com/?s=ibrox+confidential.

Rangers Tax Case. 'My Blog Shows how Scotland's Media were Complicit in Rangers' Fall.' Last modified 17 February 2012. http://www.guardian.co.uk/football/blog/2012/feb/17/scotland-media-rangers.

Rangers Tax Case. 'Wrapping It All Up.' Last modified 30 July 2012. http://rangerstaxcase.wordpress.com/2012/07/30/wrapping-it-all-up.

Reinardy, Scott, and Wayne Wanta. *The Essentials of Sports Reporting*. Routledge, 2009.

Segal, Mark. 'A Tending Topic.' Last modified 7 June 2011. http://www.wsc.co.uk/content/view/5434/38.

Spiers, Graham. 'Ecstasy and Agony of Rangers Fans'. Last modified 15 February 2012. http://www.scotsman.com/the-scotsman/opinion/comment/graham-spiers-ecstasy-and-agony-for-rangers-fans-1-2119018.

Telegraph Editorial. 'Lancashire Telegraph Comment: Time to Go Steve Kean.' Last modified 19 December 2011.
http://www.lancashiretelegraph.co.uk/sport/9427073.Lancashire_Telegraph_comm ent__Time_to_go_Steve.

Temple, Mick. *The British Press*. Open University Press, 2008.

Thompson, Alex. 'Rangers: How come Nobody Saw this Coming.' Last modified 5 April 2011.
http://blogs.channel4.com/alex-thomsons-view/rangers-coming/1088.

Something's Amiss in Football's Home: Fandom, Media Saturation and Community

Katharine Jones

Abstract

Drawing on semi-structured interviews with 120 fans of different football clubs in England, as well as some football journalists, I examine why some feel so disaffected and disillusioned by the current state of football and fan communities. The fans, interviewed over a ten year period, had diverse reasons for supporting a club and diverse definitions of fandom (from season ticket holders, to "sky sports fans" who had never seen a live game), but their disillusionment extended beyond the fortunes of their own club or the national team to include the state of football fandom in general. Fan culture has clearly been transformed by the changes wrought since the Taylor Report. However, the mediated spectacle with wall-to-wall television, radio and internet coverage has led some fans to pull back from the game and reassess the role it plays in their lives. They explained their increasing disenchantment by referencing both money and media saturation. Some felt that money, while revolutionising their viewing experience, has turned the sport into a 'product' and them into 'consumers.' Fans who regurgitate what they read, see or hear in the tabloids, television or radio were also frustrating to my interviewees. Callers to phone-ins or commenters on football blogs came in for particular criticism, with some fans characterising them as 'mentally ill.' This paired with anger about journalistic 'churn' and ideas getting repeated in different contexts until they seem true makes some fans feel that football is no longer the game they once loved. Although tribalism and localism are still important, a growing number of fans are disillusioned because football has retreated from its local roots while the loudest, media-driven fans get all the attention.

Key Words: Commodification of football, football fandom, disaffection of fans, media saturation, fans as consumers, corporatisation of football.

*****

1. Introduction

We all know that English football is becoming more and more of a commodity, as the profit potential of the game has expanded with the Sky money, foreign owners, the wages earned by players, and the media-fuelled soap operas of Ashley and Cheryl, and Colleen and Wayne, et cetera.

I have interviewed 120 fans of the game over the last decade, and have begun to see a new kind of disillusionment explicitly emerging. Although in the early 2000s, fans complained about inauthentic armchair fans, glory hunters, and out-of-towners, the discontent I have seen more recently seems to suggest a different kind of rupture in the football community. Not only do fans seem angrier about the state of football, but I have found more of them who have decided to pull back from fandom because they cannot stand the direction in which the game is heading.

2. Commodification of Football and Media Saturation: Where Are the Fans Going?

In England, fan culture has clearly been transformed by the changes wrought since Hillsborough and the Taylor Report.[1] Many scholars of the game have discussed the effects of these changes – in terms of all-seater stadia, price increases, and a different kind of atmosphere.[2] Guilianotti conceptualises some of these changes in terms of commodification, suggesting that the '*flaneur*' is becoming the 21st century model of fandom – a cool cosmopolitan dilettante who prefers to consume football through virtual reality like television and the internet, rather than experience the heat of a traditional supporter's unmediated fandom. He ends this article with a warning that if supporters continue to lose out, there will be no football fandom left for the *flaneur* to consume.[3]

I tend to revert to Anderson's[4] idea of an 'imagined community' of fandom when I examine my data. (And, apologies to Giulianotti, but I'm not prepared to give up the word 'fan,' so I use it as a catch all term when people define themselves as following, loving, supporting, or being connected to football.) Every fan is different, but their sense of belonging is often so strong that it supersedes the heterogeneity that they logically know exists in their fanbase. Hence fandom seems to fit well into the idea of community that continually gets reimagined by fans, even though they will never meet every other fan. We see this when fans use 'we' to talk their club; they unabashedly believe that they and fellow fans *are* the club; players, managers, even owners, may be 'we' at the moment, but they come and go, unlike loyal fans who supposedly stay through thick and thin.

And yet my data suggest that some fans are not staying through thick and thin. As Giulianotti warned, fans are increasingly turned off by the very aspects of 21st century fandom that attracted *flaneurs*.[5] Specifically, the commodification of football, and the saturated media coverage are starting to grate. While some fans keep supporting, obsessing, and following their clubs, others are checking out of the commodified mediated spectacle that football now is.

Some media scholars suggest that the internet and social media have enhanced fan communities, so that 'virtual' or 'portable' communities allow people from all over the world (or next door) to commune with each other over their common love of a club.[6] Many of these scholars see technology as a way to insert energy back into our flagging sense of community. Even the fan complaints that we see in research on online fan forums show that the online world helps to reassert a sense of community.[7] Obviously the online world complicates notions of community to a huge extent.

However, some of the fans I interviewed have begun to explicitly exclude themselves from the community of fans as corporatisation and media saturation change its values. Their sense of alienation and anomie seems to come from shifts in what Appadurai calls the 'regimes of value.'[8] Their ideas about fandom are so different from the imagined community that that they cannot even imagine themselves being part of it anymore. Unlike AFC Wimbledon or FCUM, they are not forming new clubs.[9] Instead, they are repudiating football fandom and what it means.

3. Methods

Over a ten year period (2001-2011), I carried out semi-structured interviews with 120 fans of different football clubs in England, as well as football journalists, referees, coaches and a couple of 'celebrity fans.' The fans ranged from armchair 'sky sports' fans who had never been to a live game, to season ticket holders who went to every game, home and away; and from fans who had recently converted to football, to those who had become fans while in nappies. The majority of the interviewees were white and heterosexual; 20 were Black or Asian and 15 identified as gay or lesbian. Their ages ranged from 18 to 74, with most in their 30s; half of the fans self-identified as working class, and half as middle class. Half are women and half men. I collected a purposive sample by identifying ways to reach fans who would be willing to talk to me; thus, I used the databases of the Premier League Survey at Leicester University, I advertised on the Kick It Out and Stonewall FC websites, and I used snowball sampling to use some interviewees to help me find others. I also carried out a small amount of participant-observation at football matches in England between 2001-2006.

I used a grounded theory method to analyse the data, letting the themes emerge from the responses of the interviewees. In this chapter, I will just focus on some of the more recent interviews I have done in order to highlight the frustration and tensions that seem to have emerged in the last couple of years. I also include some interviews with journalists who help to frame this disillusion.

4. Lack of Atmosphere and Passion: Plus Fans Are Priced Out

When I first began interviewing in 2002 I saw how eloquent fans were about the changes in the atmosphere, the rise of corporate boxes, and the 'ordinary folk priced out of the game' (Barry). Many referenced Roy Keane's now infamous 'prawn sandwiches' comment about people wanting to be entertained and complained about corporate boxes and a 'bank manager' type:

> who doesn't know anything about anything has been given his meal and he's there (...) because his grandson's uncle's best mate is his lawyer. Do you know what I mean? And he's got four

tickets. It doesn't make me feel good. (Jack, Black male Arsenal
fan, interviewed 2004).

Sixty one year old white Liverpool fan Victor said that 'new fans' were 'more
city (…) high tech type people' and, like other fans I interviewed in the early
2000s, he worried about whether they had the staying power he had.

These fans link the lack of atmosphere to the money that football has attracted;
this has led to 'people sitting on their hands' rather than standing, shouting, singing
and joining in to create the atmosphere the old timers remember.

5. Expectations and Entitlement of Fans, and Owners' Attitudes

These 'new' fans brought something more insidious to the game, however.
'Corporate' fans expected to win, had a sense of entitlement, because of the
monetary transaction in which they engaged. Victor felt that *they* thought:

> I can air me view because I've paid me money, even if it's
> derogatory. Whereas *I* would say I've paid me money to support
> the team even if they're playing badly. Always at Anfield, you
> [used to] appreciate the football. If the opposition played well
> they always got a big hand. But I don't think that applies to a lot
> of people now. They're not there for the football so much as the
> winning.

Journalist Gary (interviewed in 2011) explained that part of this was because
the wages had gone up so much:

> Increasingly fans seem to have this mentality of entitlement,
> where they fully expect to be dazzled week in week out by
> players (…) because these players are on such good money. But
> if a team plays badly for half an hour they get booed off at half
> time.

The behaviour of Chelsea fans and their owner was particularly galling to many
of my recent interviewees. For instance, white Liverpool fan Tom (interviewed in
2011) said:

> Actually I also lost interest in football when Abramovich came
> in. Because he spent half a billion pounds on footballers, on men
> to run round after a ball, half a billion pounds! (…) And also the
> Chelsea fans don't enjoy it, they've had their expectations raised,
> they had a couple of seasons of fun and now they call up Talk
> Sport or 606 and they say 'I'm so angry we lost (…) This isn't

the standard I've come to expect.' So you don't get any more out
of doing well, you know, you don't enjoy it.

White Spurs fan Mike (also interviewed in 2011) tried to reconcile the
behaviour of Chelsea and Manchester City owners with the fact that football is a
sport:

> I think certainly, when Abramovich, characters like that, came in
> and you've got the Man City [owners] I mean (…) what is
> football? (…) It should be a sport or a game that should be
> enjoyed both by the players and the spectators, whatever form
> they come in. You then have to say (…) is it [the] be all and end
> all to win? We now have premier teams that are there just to
> satisfy somebody's ego.

Here we can see these fans' anxiety that the hyper commodification and
commercialisation of football is actually destroying the game *as a game*. As fans
(and the owners of their clubs) turn from fans to consumers (or flaneurs), they feel
they have *bought* the right to expect results. The fans I interviewed could see the
way this attitude permeated the game. Booing your own players, refusing to
applaud the opposition, forgetting that it *is* actually a game: these were all seen as
by-products of the money in football.

6. Journalism Encourages the 'Your Team is Shit' Mentality, and 'Churn'

Aside from the fact that the 2011 interviewees were increasingly turned off by
the money in the game, I also saw media saturation emerging as a theme that made
them increasingly unhappy.

Twenty four hour news media, radio phone-ins and social media were new or
non-existent at the beginning of the decade; now, they are ubiquitous. Many fans
that I interviewed were disgusted with the ways football had invaded every aspect
of the media and internet. They often denigrated so-called fans who simply
reported back what they had heard commentators say on TV or read on the
internet. Victor, quoted earlier, had a novel idea to weed out the imposters who just
repeated what they heard in the media:

> You should take a little test, you should take 10 penalties, you
> should be forced to run with the ball and dribble with it, and
> …test your skills on the rules and regulations and then you
> should [wear] a colour:… red because you're an expert, pink
> because you failed on so much, and off-white because you're
> rubbish!

White Liverpool fan Tom used the idea of 'churnalism' to explain his disdain for social media and wall-to-wall news coverage:

> It's not real journalism, [it's multiple media outlets reproducing the same few pieces of information over and over] and it's not really helpful…it's just churning through information and (…) with Facebook and (…) Twitter (…) we've habituated ourselves to deal with life in that way and to kind of deal with this churn. We've lost the idea that we are friends and that we are meant to support (…) and love each other and we've just started to see ourselves as nodes or information providers you know.

This idea is from Guardian journalist Nick Davies's *Flat Earth News* where he found that financial constraints and the 24 hour news cycle are encouraging journalists to use press releases rather than researching and writing actual news stories.[10] Tom takes the idea to argue that fans themselves repeat the same mindless 'press releases' too in social media and in everyday conversations:

> [A colleague] would read the back of [a tabloid and whatever they] said in their ridiculous, delirious tone, he would then repeat as a kind of powerful fact. [You] can never get away from it. You go on Comment is Free or Football 365 [and it's very off-putting], it's just this kind of endless fury and people are so cross about football (…) They feel things are being done to them (…) It doesn't matter what happens next because whatever you achieve people will be angry and the only thing you are allowed to express joyfully is (…) someone else's loss.

Tom's response was to distance himself from friends, colleagues and the game itself: 'I'd just say as a mantra, 'I don't coach the team and I don't manage the team and I don't think I will ever be able to play for the team, so there's nothing that I can do.'

The journalists in particular became aware of this anger, some naming it as insanity, through the high levels of criticism they received about their work from anonymous posters and callers. As Karl, a white Arsenal fan and journalist, explained:

> People who do phone-ins are the same people who post comments on blogs (…) it's probably about five thousand people in the country who are seriously deranged and have serious personality problems and they are always the same! Because they are given so much exposure, they feel that because they are on

the air they have to say something that is going to shake them up a little bit so they will go 'uuuurgh!' [They] make a lot of noise in the grounds, (…) when they chat on phone ins, when they post comments. And they are seen, wrongly, as the core of football supporters in this country.

For Karl the core of football support was really the silent majority, rather than the noisy few who got all the attention. While one could argue that journalists have a vested interest in seeing people who disagree with them (and are filling copy) as insane, others concurred with this point of view.

Although Tom wasn't the only interviewee who had pulled away because of money and media coverage, I am going to quote him again because he links the two together with his ideas about insanity:

> [they are] mentally ill (…) very unhappy people (…) I just find it really sad that the dialogue around football is driven by obviously by capital [and] mentally ill people, people who have nothing in their lives. [They] can't get their head around this simple idea that if you continually pay forty pounds a fortnight and fifty pounds a month to Sky, that is why [players] earn that amount of money. You cannot be angry about that amount of money because you are giving it to them. [It's] really really insane.

In *The Wisdom of Crowds*, Surowiecki points out that the loudest, most talkative people in a social group are often those who frame discussions and ultimately become the decision makers, whether or not their input is based on sound evidence.[11] Tom and Karl are right that the 24/7 news cycle has encouraged the loudest, media-driven fans to get all the attention.

These, and other fans I interviewed who have pulled away from the game, are doing so partly because they can't stand the ways commodification has saturated us with data about football; and they find people's responses to these data troubling. Tom raised the issues of love, support and friendship; it's sad that he and others are starting to find there is no place for them in the football community as it is currently constructed.

Notes

[1] Rt. Hon. Lord Justice P. Taylor, *The Hillsborough Stadium Disaster: Interim Report* (London: Her Majesty's Stationery Office, 1989); Rt. Hon. Lord Justice P. Taylor, *The Hillsborough Stadium Disaster: Final Report* (London: Her Majesty's Stationery Office, 1990).

[2] John Bale, 'The Changing Face of Football: Stadiums and Communities,' *Soccer and Society* 1 (2000): 91-101; Richard Giulianotti, *Football: A Sociology of the Global Game* (Cambridge and Oxford: Polity Press. 2000); Anthony King, *The End of the Terraces* (Leicester: Leicester University Press 2002); Tim Crabbe and Adam Brown, '"You're not Welcome Anymore": The Football Crowd, Class and Social Exclusion,' in *British Football and Social Exclusion*, ed. S. Wagg (New York and London: Routledge 2004), 26-46.

[3] Richard Giulianotti, 'Supporters, Followers, Fans and *Flaneurs:* A Taxonomy of Spectator Identities in Football', *Journal of Sport & Social Issues* 26 (2002): 25-46.

[4] Benedict Anderson, *Imagined Communities* (London: Verso, 1983).

[5] Giulianotti, 'Supporters, Followers.'

[6] Mary Chayko, *Portable Communities: The Social Dynamics of Online and Mobile Connectedness* (Albany, NY: State University of New York Press, 2008); Howard Rheingold, *The Virtual Community*, revised edition (Cambridge, MA: MIT Press, 2002).

[7] Lisa Bogardus, 'The Bolt Wars: A Social Worlds Perspective on Rock Climbing and Intragroup Conflict,' *Journal of Contemporary Ethnography* XX.X (2011): 1-26; David Rowe, Andy Ruddock and Brett Hutchins. 'Cultures of Complaint: Online Fan Message Boards and Networked Digital Media Sport Communities,' *Convergence: The International Journal of Research into New Media Technologies* 16 (2010): 298-316; Andy Ruddock, '"Let's Kick Racism Out Of Football, and the Lefties Too!" Responses to Lee Bowyer on a West Ham Web Site,' *Journal of Sport & Social Issues* 29 (2005): 369-385.

[8] Arjun Appadurai, ed., *The Social Life of Things: Commodities in Cultural Perspective* (Cambridge: Cambridge University Press, 1986).

[9] Adam Brown, 'Politics, Theory and Practice. "Our Club, Our Rules": Fan Communities at FC United of Manchester,' *Soccer & Society* 9 (2008): 346-358.

[10] Nick Davis, *Flat Earth News* (London: Random House, 2009).

[11] James Surowiecki, *The Wisdom of Crowds: Why the Many are Smarter than the Few and how Collective Wisdom Shapes Business, Economies, Societies, and Nations* (New York: Doubleday, 2004).

Bibliography

Anderson, Benedict. *Imagined Communities.* London: Verso, 1983.

Appadurai, Arjun, ed. *The Social Life of Things: Commodities in Cultural Perspective.* Cambridge: Cambridge University Press, 1986.

Bale, John. 'The Changing Face of Football: Stadiums and Communities.' *Soccer and Society* 1 (2000): 91-101.

Bogardus, Lisa. 'The Bolt Wars: A Social Worlds Perspective on Rock Climbing and Intragroup Conflict.' *Journal of Contemporary Ethnography* XX (2011): 1-26.

Brown, Adam. 'Politics, Theory and Practice "Our Club, Our Rules": Fan Communities at FC United of Manchester.' *Soccer & Society* 9 (2008): 346-358.

Chayko, Mary. *Portable Communities: The Social Dynamics of Online and Mobile Connectedness.* Albany, NY: State University of New York Press, 2008.

Crabbe, Tim and Adam Brown. '"You're not Welcome Anymore": The Football Crowd, Class and Social Exclusion.' *British Football and Social Exclusion*, edited by S. Wagg, 26-46. New York and London: Routledge, 2004.

Davis, Nick. *Flat Earth News.* London: Random House, 2009.

Giulianotti, Richard. *Football: A Sociology of the Global Game.* Cambridge and Oxford: Polity Press, 2000.

Giulianotti, Richard. 'Supporters, Followers, Fans and *Flaneurs*: A Taxonomy of Spectator Identities in Football.' *Journal of Sport & Social Issues* 26 (2002): 25-46.

King, Anthony. *The End of the Terraces.* Leicester: Leicester University Press, 2002.

Rheingold, Howard. *The Virtual Community.* Revised Edition. Cambridge, MA: MIT Press, 2002.

Rowe, David, Andy Ruddock and Brett Hutchins. 'Cultures of Complaint: Online Fan Message Boards and Networked Digital Media Sport Communities.' *Convergence: The International Journal of Research into New Media Technologies* 16 (2010): 298-316.

Ruddock, Andy. '"Let's Kick Racism Out Of Football, and the Lefties Too!" Responses to Lee Bowyer on a West Ham Web Site.' *Journal of Sport & Social Issues* 29 (2005): 369-385.

Surowiecki, James. *The Wisdom of Crowds: Why the Many are Smarter than the Few and how Collective Wisdom Shapes Business, Economies, Societies, and Nations.* New York: Doubleday, 2004.

Taylor, Rt. Hon. Lord Justice P. *The Hillsborough Stadium Disaster: Interim Report.* London: Her Majesty's Stationery Office, 1989.

Taylor, Rt. Hon. Lord Justice P. *The Hillsborough Stadium Disaster: Final Report.* London: Her Majesty's Stationery Office, 1990.

Followers, Fans, Supporters and Flâneurs Engaging with Equality and Diversity

Roy Krøvel

Abstract
The massive Norwegian interest in British football signals profound changes in the role football plays in and for local communities and society more widely. This chapter reflects on what this means for discourses on equality and diversity. It follows the discourses of Norwegian followers, supporters, fans and flâneurs on equality and diversity to understand better how these discourses are formed and affected by the ways people organize, interact and engage with their environment.

Key Words: Fans, flâneurs, supporters, Norway.

*****

According to Richard Giulianotti, the 'broad trend in sports identification is away from the supporter model (with its hot, traditional identification with local clubs) and toward the more detached, cool, consumer-orientated identification of the flâneur'.[1] Recent studies on Norwegian fans of British clubs have questioned the dichotomy between local and hot on the one hand and distant and cool on the other. Norwegian fans of British clubs identify themselves as supporters, closely relating loyalty to a club with identification with expressions of local culture.[2]

Norwegian supporters of Manchester United, for instance, eagerly debate 'how many foreigners United should have' in the team (thread on forum.united.no). All the participants in the debate seem to agree that 'being a local lad' matters, although the definition of 'being local' varies. A few argue that being Irish should count as British in this context, especially considering the value and importance Irish players have had for United over the last few years. Ryan Giggs is also a cause for concern, as he is Welsh. Nonetheless, 'he is as good as a local lad, if you ask me', says Cristiano R. (22 October 2008). 'I don't understand what place of birth has got to do with it? What matters is what goes on inside his head (how he has been formed as a person, who he is, where he has become a man, where his heart lies, and so forth', adds Colina (22 October 2008). Walter Crickmer does not agree (22 October 2008). 'In my opinion, birthplace matters a lot for the question of being local or not. That's just how I feel. And that's why Scholes is much more local than Giggs, although I do understand why Giggs is seen as local in a way.'

When arguing for the value of a local team consisting mostly of 'local lads', the members of the forum draw explicitly on their own backgrounds and experiences from (mostly) small Norwegian villages. The strange thing, however, on which nobody comments, is that they themselves, as foreigners, would be excluded from the very imagined community of locals which they promote as the foundation for a future Manchester United.

Giulianotti develops a taxonomy of four ideal-type categories to classify spectators specifically as a tool to map 'historical changes and cultural differences experienced by specific spectator communities in their relationships with identified clubs'.[3] Forms of loyalty are seen as particularly significant in order to classify and map 'kinds of identification and solidarity with the club'.[4] 'The cool consumer spectator is a football flâneur. The flâneur acquires a postmodern spectator identity through a depersonalised set of market dominated virtual relationships, particularly interactions with the cool media of television and the Internet'.[5]

1. Notes on Methodology

The research begins with a qualitative reading of approximately 140 articles published online, mainly by ordinary members of Volda fotballklubb (VTI fotball) (http://www.vti-fotball.no). It then proceeds by following the online debate among members of three of the largest Norwegian organisations of supporters of British clubs (http://www.chelsea.no/; http://www.liverpool.no/; http://www.united.no/), in addition to the umbrella organisation, 'Union of Norwegian supporters of British football': http://www.supporterunionen.com/.

2. Engaging with Equality and Diversity

Recent research on football and fandom in Norway indicates that a profound transformation has been taking place over the last few years. When Vålerenga played Manchester United in Oslo in August 2012, for instance, Norwegian newspapers reported that most spectators went home disappointed because their favourite team was 'held to a goalless draw'.[6] The interesting point here is that the disappointed spectators did not support the local team Vålerenga, but the foreign team, Manchester United. In fact, the largest Norwegian organisations of supporters of Norwegian teams struggle to recruit 1000 members while Manchester United Supporters' Club, Scandinavia (MUSCS) (run from Norway) has 43,000 members.[7] This is a general trend. Local or national organisations struggle to maintain a diminishing membership base while organisations of supporters of British clubs have increased their membership significantly over the last three to four decades. This shifts the social context of the discourses on equality and diversity away from the traditional organisation where members play several roles and interact socially on a wide range of issues and on different local or national social arenas, to forums where the members are held together by one dominating issue (loyalty to a particular club) and play almost exclusively one social role (fan or supporter). It would be naive to assume that the production of discourses on equality and diversity continues unaffected by such an important shift in the social environment.

In 2012, Liverpool's Luis Suárez was punished by the FA for abusing Manchester United's Patrice Evra during a game. The debates on the Suarez/Evra controversy are enlightening for at least two reasons. First is the massive interest and engagement it caused among fans. Second is the powerful influence loyalty seems to exert on the way supporters and fans see and evaluate the case. Among Liverpool and Manchester United supporters online a variety of arguments are found, some demanding punishment, others defending Suarez against accusations of racial abuse. The important observation for the topic of this article, however, is the apparent dominance of loyalty as a generative mechanism in the production of discourses. Among supporters of Liverpool there is consensus for the view that Suarez was a victim of injustice. I have not identified anyone raising a voice to support Evra. Among supporters of Manchester, though, the opposite obtains. All see Evra as the victim of unacceptable racial abuse. There is nearly 100 per cent correlation between loyalty and the expressed view; loyalties determine to a significant degree what fans say about norms and values.

A rather similar case illustrates this point further. In the semi-finals of the Champions League, Chelsea captain John Terry was sent off for kicking Barcelona striker Alexis Sanchez in the back. This happened in the middle of another heated debate on racial abuse, as Terry was accused of racially abusing West Ham's Anton Ferdinand. After the Barcelona game, Terry apologised to the fans for being sent off, as this meant that he would not be available for the finals.[8] The Norwegian supporters of Chelsea reacted very positively to this apology. 'John Terry is king', wrote a fan on www.chelsea.no. This soon became the most 'liked' comment on the forum. The support for Terry should be seen in the context of the controversy about racial slur – the supporters probably felt the need to defend a loyal captain. A closer look at this apology and the reaction from the Norwegian fans, however, shed additional light on the production of norms and values in this community of fans. Terry apologised for letting teammates and Chelsea fans down. From an ethical point of view, however, an apology for kicking an opponent in the back should really go to the victim of the kicking, not to the club or the fans. But this was absent from the discussion, after the game, among Norwegian fans of Chelsea, in which supporters, interacting only with other supporters, do not attempt to discuss the ethics of the kicking in light of some notion of universal rights. What is 'right' is 'right' because it will help or benefit the team *we* support.

This finding can be further analysed through a perspective presented by Bauman.[9] A 'cloakroom community' is a place where 'people gather before a two-hour performance to hang their anoraks or cloaks (...). They are put together, temporarily, around a shared focus. There are little lateral bonds between the gathered, either extant or emergent apart of that focus of fleeting interest'.[10] The interaction online between Norwegian supporters of British clubs related to these particular issues of equality and diversity appears to be largely the product of a 'depersonalised set of market dominated virtual relationships, particularly interactions with the cool media of television and the Internet'.[11] The type of discursive production found in these cases certainly also brings to mind arguments against the corruptive powers of capitalism and consumerism by Habermas and Adorno.[12]

3. A Capability Approach

A very different discourse on football and community exists online on the webpage of *Volda Turn og Idrottslag – Fotball* (www.vti-fotball.no). One issue, the death of a senior member, concerned the members of this community more than anything else. The article announcing his death was followed by a long list of comments, revealing the depth of sorrow and anguish felt by most members, and a Facebook page publishing a short obituary was soon 'liked' by hundreds of members. This was by far the most important event for the club in this period. Interestingly, the member who died had a mental impairment and depended on help to function in many other life activities, but in football he had found a space where he was both very useful and appreciated. He was not the only one experiencing football in this manner.

The point here is to note the diversity and complexity of the club's activities and the communication between its members which reflects the multifaceted and complex interactions and tasks going on in a community of players, parents and followers. This is in contrast with the discussions between the supporter unions of British clubs.

The discourse takes into account the variety and diversity of capabilities among the members. Difference in capability is not treated as something threatening, but as something that can enrich the community. This is not unusual. On the contrary, the discourse reflects the ethical guidelines established by the National Football Association of Norway as part of the Fair Play programme. The guidelines deal with important aspects of football, for instance advising parents and other spectators: 'Stimulate and encourage your child to participate – don't pressure'; 'Ask if the game was fun and exciting – not just about the result'; 'Show respect for the club's work – participate in parental meetings to clarify attitudes and ambitions'; and 'Remember that the children will do as you do – not as you say'.[13]

4. A Flâneur at the Pub

A very different way of enjoying football can be experienced at a large number of pubs that show games on television screens while serving beer and other drinks. A relatively large group of such spectators came to watch the games between Mexico and Japan, and Brazil and South Korea, at O'Reilly's, on television, on 7 August 2012. My main interest was to observe those moments in the games that caused excitement and emotional engagement.

I found several types of moments in the games that caused particularly strong reactions among the spectators. The diversity and variety of those moments is important. Early in one of the games I noticed strong reactions when a player was injured. The reaction did not come immediately, but a few moments later when the situation was replayed in slow motion and we could see clearly that the player had landed awkwardly, injuring his ankle. We also noticed the agony on his face as he realised his injury, agony that was reflected on the faces of the spectators in the pub. For me, at least, it was not an intellectual interpretation of the signs and symbols that resulted in my *feeling* his agony, but, rather, a non-verbal bodily form of communication that awoke memories of real pain experienced during my own 'career' as a footballer. Seeing the injury happening in slow motion caused me real bodily pain – and a similar type of reaction was visible on the faces of the other spectators in the room. We are suffering beings, according to Sayer and Vetlesen.[14] The reaction of the spectators in the pub illustrates why pain and agony can be seen as universal human experiences which can potentially help us understand and empathise with others.[15]

Second, the spectators reacted with displays of joy and pleasure at moments during the games. The spectators supporting one of the teams and the seemingly neutral spectators did not necessarily display joy and pleasure at the same moments, however. The supporters of particular teams reacted most strongly when someone scored a goal or when it looked as if someone had a real opportunity to score. The neutral spectators also seemed to enjoy these moments of intense passion, but also displayed pleasure through outbursts of smiles and exuberant shouts at other moments. One yelled to his friends around a table, 'Did you see that?' Yes, they all did. It was a beautiful *move* by one of the Mexican players. 'Good balance!' he added, demonstrating with his hand in the air. To understand such reactions, we must go beyond the traditional forms of hermeneutics. According to Sonntag, 'in place of a *hermeneutics* we need an *erotics* of art'.[16] It is, I believe (based on the observation of spectators without any particular bond of loyalty to any team), possible to enjoy football simply because beautiful movements are a source of pleasure.

If this group of spectators had to be categorised according to Giulianotti's taxonomy, they would probably have to be described as 'flâneurs'. They could possibly be said to be buying into some kind of authenticity – at the least an interest in sharing the experience of seeing and enjoying the game with fans loyal to the teams playing. While this particular experience is closely related to 'interactions with the cool media of television and the Internet, understanding these spectators mainly as cool consumers or as somehow pursuing to 'acquire a postmodern spectator identity through a depersonalised set of market dominated virtual relationships', makes it difficult to understand and interpret many aspects of this particular form of spectatorship.[17] To understand the multiple ways in which people enjoy football and find involvement with it valuable, we need to draw on a broader understanding of what it means to be a human. The capability approach of

Sen and Nussbaum can enrich the analysis to include perspectives in addition to those related to loyalty and postmodern consumerism.

Still, consumerism continues to permeate Norwegian football. Former membership-run clubs are now registered companies owned by capitalists. Owners wield increasing influence over the hiring and firing of managers and coaches.[18] Some groups of supporters resign themselves to hoping that some 'rich uncle' with money to spend will buy the club and purchase new players. Increasingly, even the most steadfast supporters begin to speak the language of commercialisation, adapting to the new reality. The spokesperson of Klanen, arguably the best-known organisation of supporters in Norway, recently had to employ the discourse of postmodern consumerism to get his point across during a protest against extravagant Americanised half-time entertainment. The club should listen to the opinion of the most dedicated supporters, he argued, for ignoring them could endanger the commercial value of the home games. 'We are the product the club is selling,' he argued.[19] Giulianotti asks what would happen if the supporter becomes a flâneur? It would, he concludes, undermine the mythological working class experience the flâneur is paying for. The spokesperson for Klanen elucidates the dilemma: the half-time entertainment is designed to attract less committed supporters and flâneurs but at the same time the 'mindless stupidity' of the entertainment threatens to drive away the most dedicated supporters. If that happened, the club would lose both the supporters and the flâneurs.

5. Conclusions

Kjernen, supporters of Rosenborg, recently launched a campaign to collect money to avoid 'bankruptcy'. The campaign letter explains that only a 'few years ago' Kjernen had 2,500 members. Today the membership has fallen 'below 1000'.[20] Organisations struggling in vain to sustain their memberships are a broad trend in Norway and the difficulties experienced by Kjernen are therefore not unusual. In light of the massive interest in British clubs, however, the development signals profound changes in the role football plays in and for local communities and society more widely. This will undoubtedly affect future discourses on equality and diversity.

Notes

[1] Richard Giulianotti, 'Supporters, Followers, Fans, and Flaneurs,' *Journal of Sport & Social Issues* 26, no. 1 (2002).
[2] Hans Hognestad, 'Transglobal Scandinavian? Globalization and the Contestation of Identities in Football,' *Soccer and Society* 10 (2009); Hans Hognestad, *Norway between Bergen and Middlesbrough: Football Identities in Motion* (Norwegian University of Sport and Physkical Education, 2004); Arve Hjelseth, *Mellom Børs,*

Katedral Og Karneval ~ *Norske Supporteres Forhandlinger Om Kommersialisering Av Fotball* (Bergen: Universitetet i Bergen, 2006).

[3] Giulianotti, 'Supporters, Followers, Fans, and Flaneurs.'

[4] Ibid., 30, 31.

[5] Ibid., 38.

[6] Jamel Rake, 'Uniteds Stjernegalleri Sløste Mot Vif', in *VG* (2012), http://www.vg.no/sport/fotball/engelsk/artikkel.php?artid=10052211.

[7] Manchester United Supporters Club Scandinavian Branch, 'Skandinavias Største Supporterklubb,' http://www.united.no/united/supporterklubben/om_supporterklubben.

[8] 'John Terry Apologises to Chelsea's Fans after Dismissal,' in *BBC* (2012). http://www.bbc.co.uk/sport/0/football/17835147.

[9] Zygmunt Bauman, *Consuming Life* (Cambridge: Polity, 2007).

[10] Mark Deuze, 'Interview with Zygmunt Bauman (Part Iii),' in *Deuzeblog: Personal Irregular Blog on Research, Teaching, Media Life Work Play* (Mark Deuze, 2007).

[11] Giulianotti, 'Supporters, Followers, Fans, and Flaneurs.'

[12] David Inglis, 'Theodor Adorno on Sport: The Jeu D'esprit of Despair,' in *Sport and Modern Social Theorists*, ed. Richard Giulianotti (New York: Palgrave Macmillan, 2004); William J. Morgan, 'Habermas on Sports: Social Theory from a Moral Perspective,' in *Sport and Modern Social Theorists*, ed. Richard Giulianotti (New York: Palgrave Macmillan, 2004).

[13] The Norwegian Football Association (NFF), 'Fair Play,' *Norway Cup*, http://www.norwaycup.no/article.php?id=1487&p=.

[14] R. Andrew Sayer, *Why Things Matter to People: Social Science, Values and Ethical Life* (Cambridge, UK ; New York: Cambridge University Press, 2011); Arne Johan Vetlesen, *A Philosophy of Pain* (London: Reaktion Books, 2010).

[15] Roy Bhaskar, *Scientific Realism and Human Emancipation* (London: Routledge, 2009).

[16] Susan Sontag, *Against Interpretation, and Other Essays* (New York; New York: Farrar, Straus & Giroux ; Distributed by Holtzbrinck Publishers, 2007), 23.

[17] Giulianotti, 'Supporters, Followers, Fans, and Flaneurs,' 38.

[18] Nicolay A. Ramm, 'Slik Vil Han Gjenreise Lillestrøm,' *VG* 24.11 (2011).

[19] Kjellsen, TV2 Nyhetskanalen, 25 June 2012.

[20] Kjernen, 'Kjernen Lurer På, ' Kjernen, http://www.kjernen.com/; Styret i Kjernen, 'Innsamlingsaksjon for Kjernen,' Kjernen, http://www.kjernen.com/index.php?option=com_content&view=article&id=3208:i nnsamlingsaksjon-for-kjernen.

Bibliography

Bauman, Zygmunt. *Consuming Life*. Cambridge: Polity, 2007.

Bhaskar, Roy. *Scientific Realism and Human Emancipation*. London: Routledge, 2009.

Deuze, Mark. 'Interview with Zygmunt Bauman (Part Iii).' In *Deuzeblog. Personal Irregular Blog on Research, Teaching, Media Life Work Play*. Mark Deuze, 2007.

Giulianotti, Richard. 'Supporters, Followers, Fans, and Flaneurs.' *Journal of Sport & Social Issues* 26, no. 1 (2002): 25-46.

Hjelseth, Arve. *Mellom Børs, Katedral Og Karneval ~ Norske Supporteres Forhandlinger Om Kommersialisering Av Fotball*. Universitetet i Bergen, 2006.

Hognestad, Hans. *Norway between Bergen and Middlesbrough: Football Identities in Motion*. Norwegian University of Sport and Physkical Education, 2004.

Hognestad, Hans. 'Transglobal Scandinavian? Globalization and the Contestation of Identities in Football.' *Soccer and Society* 10 (2009): 358-373.

Inglis, David. 'Theodor Adorno on Sport: The Jeu D'esprit of Despair.' In *Sport and Modern Social Theorists*, edited by Richard Giulianotti. New York: Palgrave Macmillan, 2004.

BBC. 'John Terry Apologises to Chelsea's Fans after Dismissal.' 2012. http://www.bbc.co.uk/sport/0/football/17835147.

Kjernen. 'Kjernen Lurer På.' *Kjernen*. http://www.kjernen.com/.

Manchester United Supporters Club Scandinavian Branch. 'Skandinavias Største Supporterklubb.' http://www.united.no/united/supporterklubben/om_supporterklubben.

Morgan, W. J. 'Habermas on Sports: Social Theory from a Moral Perspective.' In *Sport and Modern Social Theorists*, edited by Richard Giulianotti. New York: Palgrave Macmillan, 2004.

Rake, Jamel. 'Uniteds Stjernegalleri Sløste Mot Vif.' In *VG*, 2012. http://www.vg.no/sport/fotball/engelsk/artikkel.php?artid=10052211.

Ramm, Nicolay A. 'Slik Vil Han Gjenreise Lillestrøm.' *VG* 24.11 (2011).

Sayer, Andrew, R. *Why Things Matter to People: Social Science, Values and Ethical Life*. Cambridge and New York: Cambridge University Press, 2011.

Sontag, Susan. *Against Interpretation, and Other Essays*. New York: Farrar, Straus & Giroux, distributed by Holtzbrinck Publishers, 2007.

Styret i Kjernen. 'Innsamlingsaksjon for Kjernen,' *Kjernen*, http://www.kjernen.com/index.php?option=com_content&view=article&id=3208:i nnsamlingsaksjon-for-kjernen.

The Norwegian Football Association (NFF). 'Fair Play.' *Norway Cup*, http://www.norwaycup.no/article.php?id=1487&p.

Vetlesen, Arne Johan. *A Philosophy of Pain*. London: Reaktion Books, 2010.

'Get out of Our Club, you Lying B*stards, Get out of Our Club': A Study of Fans, Football and Ownership in England

Deirdre Hynes and Kate Themen

Abstract
This chapter examines transformations in the football match-day experience in the Premier League era in order to evaluate the manner in which commercial imperatives intersect with supporters and the critical narratives that emerge. Drawing upon survey data gathered from members of the Spirit of Shankly Supporters Union, AFC Liverpool and supporters of Liverpool FC, the chapter demonstrates that supporter narratives are indicative of the way in which patters of 'traditional' support are complicated by the extension of corporate governance to locally based communal focal points such as football clubs.

Key Words: Football, supporters, supporters' union, Spirit of Shankly.

*****

1. Introduction

The match-day experience has undergone significant changes in the Premier League era, producing a dialectical relationship between commercial imperatives and supporter interests. The critical narratives that emerge at the intersection of those countervailing forces offer a useful basis for understanding the scope and implications of developments that have transformed the face of the modern game. Drawing upon Richard Giulianotti's supporter taxonomy[1] and the concept of 'Disneyisation',[2] we situate the tendency for football clubs to conflate *supporters* with *consumers* and emergence of associated cultural practices that are considered to be antithetical to traditional patterns of support[3] as examples of commodification. We then consider the oppositional responses articulated in interviews and surveys conducted with members of Spirit of Shankly Supporters Union, AFC Liverpool and supporters of Liverpool FC who regularly attended games in the pre- and post-Premier League era. Their perspectives facilitate a discussion that uses the match-day experience as a lens through which to view the changing nature of supporter communities. Consequently, we argue that supporter narratives are indicative of the way in which patterns of 'traditional' support are complicated by the extension of corporate governance to locally based communal focal points.

2. Supporters vs. Consumers

Critical supporter narratives are hardly a new phenomenon in football.[4] Russell[5] and Taylor[6] have demonstrated that class divisions and 'protests'[7] existed prior to increased broadcast interest that developed in the early nineties. However, the terms of dissention shifted after 1992 as *BskyB* television's involvement triggered growing concerns about the commodification and consequent gentrification of the game. This perception led to numerous politicised fan protests[8] over a general dissatisfaction with the match-day experience,[9] the introduction of fractured kick-off times scheduled to satisfy television broadcasting, and increased ticket prices put match-day attendance out of reach for segments of the traditional support base. The consequence of which has been the marginalisation of collective identities that traditionally emerged through supporter engagement.[10] Thus, the pursuit of the trans-national football market has resulted in a loss of 'local' identities and fan communities and produced perceptions of the 'sanitisation' of traditional football ethnologies.[11]

Movements or patterns of protest mobilised around a categorical definition of 'tradition' are premised on the idea that pre-1992 football networks sustain greater resonance and meaning than do newly emerged (and emerging) football communities. Inherent tensions belie the temporal and complex nature of supporter communities. As we extend the local/global dichotomy to our analysis, we identify two key categorisations from Giulianotti's taxonomy. Traditional *supporters* are those who have familial ties to their club and a long-term emotional investment, further reflected in a pattern of 'thick communities' that may also include economic investment through purchase of season tickets, away support, and so forth. The antithesis of the supporter is the *flâneur*. Taken from Baudelaire's urban social type first chronicled in the 19th century, the football flâneur is characterised by distant, non-reciprocal ties. Social bonds are weak and, for the purposes of our research, this type of relationship between traditional football supporters and a football club is of particular interest. Contradictions become apparent as we investigate the relationship between 'traditional' supporters and 'marginal' participatory spectators because of the necessity of attracting 'consumer' football fans in a commercially driven football context.

The spending power of the flâneur makes him/her a highly sought after, potential customer of various products. In that sense the flâneur is embraced by many local supporters of bigger clubs as they realise that in a neo-liberal environment, the club needs the income generated by attracting wealthy cosmopolitan flâneurs.[12] Such tensions were expressed through our interview data:

> It's a global club with Scouse heart…'what do you do to support the club?', some might buy the shirt, some might go to every game because they're local, you'll have someone in Australia who'll get up at 4 o'clock (am) every Saturday morning to watch…who's the better fan?[13]

This question not only problematises the definition of supporter 'authenticity' it also references the particularising tendencies outlined by Robertson, which reveal the point at which the global meets the local.[14] In the context of protest then, it becomes apparent that supporters' relationship to the commercialising tendencies of contemporary football governance is intersected by the necessity of generating and maintaining a global fanbase in order to elevate the club brand.

In terms of locating change and the perceived loss of 'authenticity' located in pre-1992 supporter networks, this process of change becomes more apparent in the following interviews. When asked to locate 'when football changed', many supporters cited the influence of satellite and now digital broadcasting as a negative facet of the contemporary game. Moreover, many respondents articulated a growing sense of disaffection with the commercial facets of English football. Of 42 respondents, 38 made reference to the central presence of money as a primary factor in undermining traditional football networks. We asked what respondents would they change about football if they could. There were issues raised that reflected a sense of tradition and shared ownership, within which supporters are positively positioned. In addition to 'gate-sharing',[15] there was a demand for the 'draft system to balance out financial differentials. Go back to a European Cup for only champions. The current set up is tedious and only makes the rich richer.'[16] Another participant called for 'more even distribution of money throughout the leagues. Limit on foreign players. Financial fair play. Supporter ownership. Money is ruining the game!'[17]

The issues of governance that inform experience of contemporary football are an evocative commentary that illustrate the extent to which commercialisation intersects with supporters and their experience of English football. By the very use of the concept of 'tradition', perceptions of the *global game* are indicative of the manner in which supporters are affected at the local level. Saturated television coverage of games undermines the importance of individual football matches for example. Therefore, emergent themes from interview data focussed specifically on the symptoms of commercial strategising that circumvent immediately practical issues for supporters, such as increases in ticket prices. These are notable issues, because they identify the manner in which structural changes intersect with our respondents' experience of the game, and the extent to which the political-economic influence of the free-market have very real implications.

The politicised supporter groups that emerged in response may then be engaged in a transformative process that seeks to affect the overall structural imbalance and redefine, or reassert, their position. For instance, the re-assertion of 'locality' at FC United is an endeavour to counteract the popular assumptions of Manchester United fans as 'plastic' or 'glory hunters' by relocating notions of *authentic* cultural practice associated with the traditional local city based rivalry.[18] Equally, at AFC Liverpool, the club's establishment is indicative of attempts to re-engage with locality and 'reclaim' the match-day experience. The chairman of AFC Liverpool observed that:

> Top flight football has generally been taken away from the
> normal fan. I mean years ago people just used to wake up and
> decide whether they wanted to go to the match or not...we
> wanted something that was our own, so as Liverpool fans we set
> one (a football club) up.[19]

The establishment of the Spirit of Shankly (SoS) Supporters Union to contest moves by businessmen Tom Hicks and George Gillett[20] to acquire Liverpool FC is indicative of the critical response generated by supporters in the face of commodification. As one member of SoS explained, football clubs are 'multi-million pound organisations based in local communities. Their position is very unique and that uniqueness is something that's forgotten about by the powers that be.'[21] Such supporter critiques struggle to gain traction against the trajectory of unregulated[22] commercialisation and ideological approaches that have become entrenched and normalised in the Premier League via the discourse of the 'free market' and consumer choice.

In its most basic terms, the balance between the structural governance and the capacity of football supporters to effect change through protest is an interesting debate. The question remains as to whether the extent to which corporate strategy has become so embedded within the English game, if it is in fact at all achievable to realign consumer focussed discourse with a philosophy that reflects the sociality of football clubs as communal focal points. The question emerges regarding the extent to which fans themselves are complicit within the process of globalisation and consequent monetisation of the Premier League. Amid the contests that prevailed during the establishment of FC United, Brown observes that, 'The fragility of oppositional fan communities [at FC United] was exposed under the weight of the corporate takeover of the club . . . some of those still attending Old Trafford have been particularly antagonistic to FCUM and its supporters'[23]

The complexities and contradictions inherent within the global and commercial growth of English football, reveals a level of complicity that problematises the position of local, traditional supporter groups. As an SoS representative explained:

> It is funny that the major problem came from our supporters
> rather than from outsiders, you know you'd expect to be attacked
> by the club, you'd expect to be attacked by people from outside
> the area saying oh it's them Scousers again, when in actual fact it
> was ourselves.[24]

He continued 'watch[ing] Man United sail off into the sunset, league titles, making massive amounts of money, Chelsea had Abramovich, Arsenal winning league titles, and we wanted our share of the pie, there's no two ways about that.'[25] Such responses to structural changes and emergent models of ownership would seem to 'legitimise'[26] the broader corporate governance of the game. For supporter protests, however, it is interesting note the extent to which corporate governance gives utility to supporters' concerns in the context of the match-day experience. Corporate governance intersects in a tangible manner for many supporters, and the requisite critiques are illustrated explicitly in a romanticised narrative that depicts pre-Premier League and post-Premier League football in a simplified dichotomous, antithetical relationship.

3. Transformations in the Match-Day Experience: Liverpool FC Match Day Memories

Transformations in the match-day experience further exemplify the extension of commercial practices. This plays out at the most basic level in the positioning and architecture of stadia, which in turn, shape the physical experience of *going* to the match. With the proclivity for contemporary new-build stadia to be located outside of traditional inner-city neighbourhoods, the match-day routine is displaced by the technical organisation designed to ease flows of supporters going to and from the match.[27] This is augmented by efforts to generate commercial revenues by theming space and fandom through a process that Dixon calls 'Disneyisation'.[28] This branding of space around stadia extends further the influence of corporate objectives over the match-day experience because it signifies the service-based, cultural and symbolic economy[29] that seeks to encompass traditional, locally based supporters and adherent identities within a commercial environment.

Responses to the online survey, which tapped memories associated with the match-day experience, featured critical assessments of commercialisation and corporate governance. The juxtaposition of such recollections with the discourses surrounding contemporary match-day experiences and stadia lends context to critical narratives. As such, memories of football during the 1970s and 1980s explicitly position the football 'experience' in a pre/post-Taylor matrix. As one respondent recalled:[30]

> My first memory of The Kop was going in when the gates opened with ten minutes to go, and there were little swarms of youths waiting to go in. And when I climbed the steps into this immense cavern of noise and blackness and wisps of smoke I saw about a dozen lads up in the rafters, just sat on girders looking out at this illuminated square of bright green with fellas running about on it. I thought whatever is going on out there must be important for those lads to climb up there to get a look at it. It was a second round league cup-tie against West Brom, so I suppose it was.[31]

Another respondent's recollections were equally evocative of a full-sensory experience of the stadium space and the intense emotions it stirred:

> The stink of p*ss on the Kop,
> Leeds being quite good and very hated,
> ManYoo fans being a bunch of violent thugs,
> Pitches in horrific condition,
> ManYoo in division two,
> Crying my eyes out when Shanks left.[32]

As indicators of a homogenised sense of identity linked to place, these reflective narratives underscore the importance of routines that lend tangibility and depth to sentiments accompanying the traditional match-day experience.[33] According to Bale, ritualised, frequently violent, aggressive, behaviour linked to identification of place fosters *civic pride* in the form of a 'celebration of community, displaying strong forms of local identification and an equally strong tendency to denigrate other (opposing) communities, by means of songs, chanting, graffiti etc.'.[34]

> Away from Anfield, I remember the threat of violence all the time. I'm sure it was at Anfield as well but I just noticed it more at other grounds – maybe because you felt a bit more exposed being in fewer numbers etc.'[35]

The experience of match days present a focus from which there emerge issues indicative of the way in which consumerist imperatives and broadcast technologies intersect at a grounded level with supporters. Where Nick Hornby's *Fever Pitch* is a precursor for physical change in stadia post-Hillsborough,[36] the consequent cultural transformation of the match day experience has served to atomise the individual and privatise public space. To such an extent, the traditional patterns of cultural practice have become excluded or marginalised. For example, the spatial dynamics of spectatorship on terraces were fluid and communal; physical proximity to fellow supporters and individual space was ill defined, and on a full terrace indistinguishable. Memories of the match-day experience generate evocative narratives that locate supporters in a fixed sense of place and traditional supporter networks. One respondent recalled:

> Going where you want on The Kop, getting brave enough to no longer sit on the bars but to go into the middle where you could sing, and then the ultimate feeling of confidence when you would start some of the songs. The squeeze at the top of the steps, the

scallies climbing over the wall to walk down the disused crumbly steps alongside.'[37]

Another respondent reminisced that:

The metal posts/barriers on the kop that were like mini goalposts without the nets in, first time I ever stood on the Kop I went with my dad and I positioned myself right behind one of them so that I could lever myself up to get a better view (being about 7 in that crowd meant that you saw feck all otherwise). Bad mistake though. The minute there was any excitement in the game the crowd surged forwards for a better look and if you were stood against the barrier, you were trapped and crushed. I never made that mistake again. The fun/downside of not standing near one was that when the crowd did surge, you'd likely end up standing 30 yards from your original spec. I lost my dad a few times when that happened.[38]

These responses suggest that the temporal facets of supporter identities and networks are immune to change. In contrast, the function of post-1989 all seating-stadia exemplify the underlying commercial imperatives driving football. Returning to Giulianotti's taxonomy, these recollections position a sense of 'tradition' in a context that is rooted in a deeply nostalgic sense of that which is *in the past*. On subsequent transformations then, the match day experience reflected in the responses below, evaluate change (and loss of *tradition*) in the dissipation of pre-1992 community networks. One participant declared that, 'Working class and youth have been priced out of top-level football. Game has been gentrified. All-seater stadiums have killed a lot of the atmosphere'[39] Another participant lamented that 'Watching a match became more expensive than supposedly elitist pastimes such as a night at the theatre.'[40]

Such reference to elitism and working class cultural practices articulate a sense of tradition that focuses on the issue of gentrification which is perceived to have purged convention. This is partially a result of transformations in the physical structure of football stadia that marginalises the position of 'authentic' working-class cultural practices. Contemporary stadia are highly disciplinary spaces that atomise the individual. Bale argues that contemporary football stadia are 'carceral' spaces, which are regulated and increasingly surveyed, facilitating a culture of passivity.[41] However, Russell has outlined the 'substantial' middle class representation at football matches prior to the twenty-year period we are discussing in this chapter.[42] These dynamics are illustrative of the complexities associated with defining traditional and authentic patterns of support, and they signal areas for further investigation.

4. Conclusion

The general consensus amongst the supporters surveyed was that unregulated commercial interests had been pursued to the detriment of traditional, *locally* based supporters. This was most evident in the elevation of prices that supporters must now pay in order to attend matches. However, many of the earlier responses outlined in this chapter are underpinned by a highly romanticised perception of their formative match-day experiences, which belies the realities of football support, particularly during the late 1970s and 1980s when English football became a European pariah. As one of our respondents was moved to note, 'away from Anfield, I remember the threat of violence all the time'. This recollection is indicative of the tensions so explicitly evident during this period. In the meantime, English football has undergone a significant transformation that has dealt with the more negative facets of being a match-day attending football supporter. But while English football's 'guardians' (the Football Association) have so fervently taken up free-market strategising, they have ignored the way the pursuit of commercial interests marginalises some sections of supporters. Perhaps this was more by design than accident, but it is notable that supporters are receptive the implications.

Notes

[1] Richard Giulianotti, 'Supporters, Followers, Fans and Flaneurs: A Taxonomy of Spectator Identities in Football,' *Journal of Sport and Social Issues* 26, 1 (2002): 25-46.

[2] Alan Bryman, *The Disneyization of Society* (London: Sage, 2004).

[3] Kevin Dixon, 'Football Fandom and Disneyization in Late Modern Life.' *Leisure Studies* iFirst article (2012): 1-21. DOI 10.1080/02614367.2012.667819.

[4] Adam Brown, '"Not for Sale"? The Destruction and Reformation of Football Communities in the Glazer Takeover of Manchester United,' *Soccer & Society* 8, No. 4 (2007): 616.

[5] David Russell, *Football and the English: A Social History of Association Football in England 1863-1995* (Preston: Carnegie Publishing, 1997).

[6] Ian Taylor, 'Football Mad: A Speculative Sociology of Soccer Hooliganism,' in *The Sociology of Sport: A Selection of Readings*, ed. Eric Dunning (London: Cass, 1971), 352-377.

[7] Taylor's discussion of football hooliganism in response to the trend towards family stands and the game as a 'spectacle'.

[8] Most notably for the purposes of this chapter, Spirit of Shankly and the formation of AFC Liverpool.

[9] Brown, '"Not for Sale"', 347.

[10] Peter Millward, *The Global Football League: Transnational Networks, Social Movements and Sport in the New Media Age* (Hampshire and New York: Palgrave Macmillan, 2011), 163.

[11] Richard Giulianotti and Roland Robertson, *Globalisation and Football* (London: Sage, 2009), 82.

[12] Hans K. Hognestad, 'Split Loyalties: Football is a Community Business,' *Soccer & Society* 13, No. 3 (2012): 383.

[13] SoS interview, May 2011.

[14] Roland Robertson, *Globalization: Social Theory and Global Culture* (London: Blackwell, 1992).

[15] Survey response 14, August 2011.

[16] Survey response 12, August 2011.

[17] Survey response 13, August 2011.

[18] Brown, '"Not for Sale"', 346.

[19] AFC Liverpool interview.

[20] Liverpool FC was again sold in October 2010 to John W. Henry's New England Sports Ventures (NESV), but not before the case ended up in the High Court as Hicks and Gillett refused to entertain NESV's £300m offer because they considered it undervalued the club. Had RBS decided to recall their loans earlier then the consequences for Liverpool Football Club could have been dramatic with the possibility of administration and deduction of league points.

[21] SoS interview.

[22] Until 1981, the FA's Rule 34 previously restricted payment of dividends to 5% of the nominal value of shares and prohibited payment to directors.

[23] Adam Brown, "Politics, Theory and Practice: "Our Club, Our Rules": Fan Communities at FC United of Manchester," *Soccer & Society* 9 (2008): 347-348.

[24] SoS interview.

[25] SoS interview.

[26] Manuel Castells, *The Information Age: Economy, Society and Culture, Volume II: The Power of Identity* (Maiden MA: Blackwell, 1997), 8.

[27] Tim Edensor and Steve Millington, 'Going to the Match: The Transformation of the Match-day Routine at Manchester City FC,' in *Staduim Worlds: Football, Space and the Built Environment*, ed. Sybelle Frank and Silke Steets (London, Routledge, 2010), 159.

[28] Dixon, 'Football Fandom'.

[29] Scott Lash and John Urry, *Economies of Signs and Space* (London: Sage, 1994), 61.

[30] From YNWA (Liverpool FC forum), January 2011.

[31] Smithdown, YNWA, January 2011.

[32] New York Red, YNWA, January 2011.

[33] Edensor and Millington, 'Going to the Match', 154.

[34] John Bale, *Sports Geography* (London: E. & F.N. Spon, 1989), 18.

[35] Charlie Clown, YNWA, January 2011.

[36] Steve Redhead, *Post Fandom and the Millennial Blues* (London: Routledge, 1997), 88.
[37] Smithdown, YNWA, January 2011.
[38] Charlie Clown, YNWA, January 2012.
[39] Survey response 1, August 2011.
[40] Survey response 2, August 2011.
[41] John Bale, 'Virtual Fandoms: Futurescapes of Football,' in *Fanatics: Power, Identity and Fandom in Football*, ed. Adam Brown (London: Routledge, 1998), 266.
[42] Russell, 1997 cited in Hognestad, 'Split Loyalties,' 378.

Bibliography

Bale, John. *Sports Geography*. London: E. & F.N. Spon, 1989.

———. 'Virtual Fandoms: Futurescapes of Football.' In *Fanatics: Power, Identity and Fandom in Football*, edited by Adam Brown, 265-277. London: Routledge, 1998.

Brown, Adam. '"Not for Sale"? The Destruction and Reformation of Football Communities in the Glazer Takeover of Manchester United.' *Soccer & Society* 8, No. 4 (2007): 614-635.

———. 'Politics, Theory and Practice: "Our Club, Our Rules": Fan Communities at FC United of Manchester.' Soccer & Society 9 (2008): 346-358.

Bryman, Alan. *The Disneyization of Society*. London: Sage, 2004.

Castells, Manuel. *The Information Age: Economy, Society and Culture, Volume II: The Power of Identity*. Maiden MA: Blackwell, 1997.

Dixon, Kevin. 'Football fandom and Disneyization in Late Modern Life.' *Leisure Studies* iFirst article (2012): 1-21. DOI:10.1080/02614367.2012.667819.

Duke, Vic. 'Local Tradition versus Globalisation: Resistance to the McDonaldisation and Disneyisation of Professional Football in England.' *Football Studies* 5, no. 1 (2002): 5-23.

Edensor, Tim and Steve Millington. 'Going to the Match: The Transformation of the Match-Day Routine at Manchester City FC.' In *Stadium Worlds: Football, Space and the Built Environment*, edited by Sybille Frank and Silke Steets, 146-162. London: Routledge, 2010.

Giulianotti, Richard. 'Supporters, Followers, Fans and Flaneurs: A Taxonomy of Spectator Identities in Football.' *Journal of Sport and Social Issues* 26, 1 (2002): 25-46.

Giulianotti, Richard, and Roland Robertson. *Globalisation and Football*. London: Sage, 2009.

Hognestad, Hans K. 'Split loyalties: football is a community business.' *Soccer & Society* 13, no. 3 (2012): 377-391.

Lash, Scott, and John Urry. *Economies of Signs and Space*. London: Sage, 1994.

Millward, Peter. *The Global Football League: Transnational Networks, Social Movements and Sport in the New Media Age*. Hampshire and New York: Palgrave Macmillan, 2011.

Redhead, Steve. *Post Fandom and the Millennial Blues*. London: Routledge, 1997.

Robertson, Roland. *Globalization: Social Theory and Global Culture*. London: Blackwell, 1992.

Russell, David. *Football and the English: A Social History of Association Football in England 1863-1995*. Preston: Carnegie Publishing, 1997.

Taylor, Ian. 'Football Mad: A Speculative Sociology of Soccer Hooliganism.' In *The Sociology of Sport: A Selection of Readings*, edited by Eric Dunning, 352-377. London: Cass, 1971.

Little United and the Big Society: Football Clubs and Community Volunteering

Annabel Kiernan and Chris Porter

Abstract
The government's Big Society vision is a source of fierce debate and controversy, particularly when set alongside severe austerity measures. This has revealed a glaring disconnect between rhetoric of empowered communities and the burgeoning reality of cuts to publicly-funded community provision. This puts pressure on organisations that rely on or promote volunteering, in financial terms through the loss of funding, but also on ideological grounds. To explore this research was conducted within the community projects of FC United of Manchester, a not-for-profit, co-operative, fan-owned, non-league football club. Findings reveal extremely positive perceptions of the community work carried out by the club, with volunteering and the ownership structure major factors in that success. Despite clear opposition to the coalition government's policies, from a community stakeholder perspective and on wider ideological grounds, the club aims to increase its capacity as a community provider, acknowledging the potential contradictions and conflicts this may bring.

Key Words: Big Society, community, co-operatives, FC United of Manchester, football, volunteering.

*****

1. Introduction

The UK government's Big Society vision is a source of fierce debate and controversy, particularly when set alongside severe austerity measures. This has revealed a glaring disconnect between rhetoric of empowered communities and the burgeoning reality of cuts to publicly-funded community provision. This puts pressure on organisations that rely on or promote volunteering, in financial terms through the loss of funding, but also on ideological grounds. To explore this issue, research was conducted within the community projects of FC United of Manchester, a not-for-profit, co-operative, fan-owned, non-league football club. Findings reveal extremely positive perceptions of the community work carried out by the club, with volunteering and the ownership structure major factors in that success. Despite clear opposition to the coalition government's policies, from a community stakeholder perspective and on wider ideological grounds, the club aims to increase its capacity as a community provider, acknowledging the potential contradictions and conflicts this may bring.

2. Research Framework

This project began as a result of an Institute for Humanities and Social Sciences Research funded project at Manchester Metropolitan University, in 2010-11. The project brief was to explore FC United as one model of co-operative social enterprise and to address the impact of co-operative activity within a local community, including questions of capacity, social value and how to define community. FC United was chosen because it represents a successful model of a co-operative Industrial and Provident Society, an organisation therefore which already operates in close alignment with the government's new economic and social priorities for the ownership, organisation and delivery of services in and by the community.

3. Data Collection

The data collection took place during the 2010-2011 football season and took the form of interviews with partner organisations and focus groups with clients and stakeholders. This included FC United volunteers and staff, community project stakeholders, partner agency staff and project participants.

4. The Big Society Context

The Big Society agenda in the UK is considered to be a rather blurry and intangible concept which has had little traction in the public arena. However, several pieces of legislation give form to its 'direction of travel'. The key legislative provisions which provide application for the concept of the Big Society are the Localism Act 2011[1] and the 'Open Public Services' White Paper.[2] Both pieces of legislation reflect the core rationale underpinning the coalition government's public service reform, which is to encourage greater diversity in the supply chain, to provide an emphasis on volunteering with a view to reducing the size and reach of government in relation to the public sector; in particular this will result in a changed role for the voluntary and community sector (VCS) while creating more room for co-operatives and social enterprises to enter a competitive market for public service contracts.

5. 'Little United'

The focus of this research is the community engagement work of Football Club United of Manchester (FC United or FC). The club was formed in 2005 by boycotting Manchester United supporters and is a fan-owned 'one member-one vote' football club. The club is internally democratic, holding annual board elections and taking resolutions from the owner-members. The club is established as a co-operative; it has approximately 3,300 members and 1270 season ticket holders. Much of the day to day work of the club is carried out by volunteers, of which in total there are around 300 registered with the club.[3] FC United currently play in the Northern Premier League (and so are three promotions away from the Football League) and ground-share with Bury FC at Gigg Lane.[4]

6. FC's Community Focus

As reflected both by the way the club was formed (through its fans' protests against Manchester United being taken into private ownership via a hostile takeover) and by the way it is constituted, FC United has established itself to be a 'community benefit' organisation. The club has embedded constitutional commitments to community working (engagement) and this in turn informs FC's approach to its own strategic development as a new football club. Notable examples of its community-led approach are: raising of £1.6million to fund a new (the club's own) ground in Moston, North Manchester, using a 'community share'[5] scheme; a legally-binding 'Asset Lock' voted in by members to ensure the new stadium remains of community benefit; and FC United were awarded 'Community Club of the Year 2012' by the Football Foundation. Consequently, FC United finds itself particularly well-placed to take advantage of the government agenda for increasing the diversity of local service supply through an enhanced role for co-operative, social enterprise, community organisations.

7. Community Projects

The community work of the football club is now firmly established, and FC United are a well-recognised partner for community working across Greater Manchester. To date, the club has had positive working partnerships with Future Jobs Fund,[6] refugee and asylum groups using football as a vehicle of community integration and cohesion, wellbeing and good neighbour projects which have emphasised reducing social isolation of older men, and football apprenticeships which assist young people to gain NVQ and other coaching qualifications. Having established a successful track record in community partnership working and successfully bidding for grant funding, FC United is now looking to expand its role as a service provider and can foresee a time when it is in a position to bid for local service contracts. In particular the new ground facility which is proposed for Moston, offers opportunities to host community sport and leisure facilities as well as social space available to local residents and FC United members and supporters.

8. FC United's Communities

One interesting issue raised by FC United's potential move into local service delivery and expanded community working is the question of whether one or more 'community' is served as a priority. So far in the club's history this underlying question has not become an immediate concern or conflict but, as the club develops, relocates and is shaped by its community commitment, it is an issue which threatens to be more prevalent in discussions about the meaning, symbolism and ultimately the identity of the club. There are clearly different definitions of community, notably of place and identity, and there are also overlapping community identities. There are some communities of identity which inform FC United and were causal in its inception: FC United fans on the whole have cultural identifications rooted in Manchester United supporter culture more generally, and the politicised anti-Glazer protests in particular.[7] Alongside that, and more so as the club develops, there are neighbourhood communities, such as the existing residential community in Moston, as well as various 'communities of disadvantage'[8] the club is committed to working with. This of course complicates the picture and brings in to sharp focus the question of what role football clubs can and should play in local service delivery.

9. Football Clubs and Their Communities: A Broader Context

It is possible to see in the way that English football was originally constituted, that ideas positioning football clubs as community actors have always been present. Particularly relevant in this context is the now defunct FA Rule 34. This rule essentially prevented football clubs from being used as a means to make money for investors by limiting the payment of dividends, something which was foreseen as a potential threat to the game, and its role in the wider community, at the time it was introduced by the Football Association in the late 19th Century.[9]

For the best part of 100 years then, football clubs were regulated to protect their community stakeholders against the perils of market forces, thus *'ensuring that clubs remain sporting institutions'*.[10] Tottenham Hotspur Football Club however, sidestepped Rule 34 in 1983 by restructuring themselves and making the football club a mere subsidiary of a larger holding company (Tottenham Hotspur PLC), which was not technically subject to the FA's rules. The Football Association's acquiescence in allowing such a fundamental rule to be disregarded by one of its member clubs allowed Manchester United to follow suit in 1991, when as a PLC it was able to pay huge dividends to its directors following flotation on the stock exchange.

This circumvention of Rule 34, and more pointedly the willingness of the game's governing body to allow football clubs to be traded as commercial concerns at the expense of more cultural and community-based stakeholders, facilitated the deregulated environment in which Malcolm Glazer would later purchase Manchester United. This of course proved the final straw for those supporters who went on to form FC United, partly in an attempt to retain or regain the community focus they felt had long been absent at their club. Of course, major football clubs and governing bodies do engage with notions of community, as is evident via the abundance of community rhetoric in official documentation, but the level and type of community engagement has been questioned as clubs are increasingly owned by absent off-shore shareholders.

Modern football governance therefore has seen clubs sidestep Rule 34 in the rush to become highly profitable commercial vehicles. Futhermore, the FA began to embrace more commercial positioning which culminated in 1992 with the establishment of the FA Premier League. From this point onwards we have seen English football clubs become truly open to the global free market and consequently there has been significant criticism of clubs, often led by fan groups, for losing touch with their local context in terms of identity, culture and community.

The commercial imperative within English football in recent years is highlighted as a factor that can easily sideline, overlook and indeed plain contradict any stated community concerns, and the prevailing tendency to view supporters as customers rather than community stakeholders again reflects the market-centred approach of many clubs.[11]

Likewise, Mellor describes contemporary English football as the '*Janus-faced sport*', pointing to the ubiquitous use of notions of community surrounding the Premier League,[12] while at the same time the reality that is its commercial imperative can render such sentiments as almost meaningless. Mellor specifically links this trend to the influence of the 'New Labour' government and its '*Third Way*' political ideology in pushing policies of social inclusion alongside a 'hands off' approach to the market, and importantly in utilising sport as a vehicle with which to engage those 'disadvantaged' communities that other, less culturally-grounded interventions often fail to reach.

It is clear – above all in their existence – that FC United recognise the contradictions in community rhetoric that act to merely soften the image of the commercially-geared Premier League. The resistance by fans to consuming the commodified product of elite football in England was of course primarily about issues of supporter culture, with a perhaps tacit understanding that a supporter-owned club could be more genuinely embedded in the local community than one owned by a financially-motivated investor.

10. Measuring Community Impact

The positioning of culture and sport as utilitarian 'means' towards the broader 'ends' of regeneration and social inclusion, as well as being debatable on various political, ethical and moral grounds[13] must also have its effectiveness questioned, though this is something that has proved notoriously difficult presumption[14] that sport, along with arts and culture generally, is good for people and communities, and is therefore well suited to deliver the qualities that are thought to be missing in certain areas, was clearly expressed in the Policy Action Team 10 report commissioned by the Labour government's Social Exclusion Unit in 1999.[15]

Community impact can often be found in less tangible qualities, for example, wellbeing. There is now an increased requirement for VCS to demonstrate social value and to calculate the social return on investment in order to secure future funding. This remains a difficult challenge and potentially highlights the difficulties for football clubs in taking on this role. In addition, football clubs like

FC United may be well-placed to enter the new market place for community service delivery but, despite very positive qualities which link them to local communities and potentially allow them to operate with more authority (because people may more readily buy into a trusted football brand) they are not immune from the same charges which are often levelled at private firms who have taken advantage of public service markets. In particular, there are questions of the training of community workers, as well as their relationship to public sector providers and community expertise extant on the ground. Further, there is a strong argument from some sections of the VCS itself that this work is niche and should therefore be based on advocacy. The question here for football clubs such as FC United as they move in to this territory is whether meeting the role requirement of a strong community organisation can be consistent with meeting the demands of the football fan communities whose priorities for their club may stand somewhat removed from the priorities of the local neighbourhood or other communities.

11. Focus Group Findings 1: Perceptions

In the focus group discussions about the role and engagement of FC United with the different client and stakeholder groups, there was an overwhelmingly positive response to the club by participants in FC's community projects. The different groups all reported feeling that their involvement with FC's community projects was good for them, that it was delivering tangible benefits to their personal development. Specifically, groups reported that they found working with FC 'enjoyable', that it engaged individuals and communities in 'healthy' activities and that for some they were developing new skills, notably for employability. It was particularly evident from the focus groups that FC United had delivered on raising aspirations, a key aim of community working and something which clearly delivers satisfaction to both client groups and community workers. It was also important to the groups interviewed for this research that 'active' engagement by FC United in local communities appeared a priority, something which set FC United aside from other football clubs involved in community work, notably Manchester United and Manchester City – as reported by one participant: 'they come to us'.

As well as delivering on core soft skills, it was reported in the discussions that FC's community engagement also offers practical help and support in organising football activities by other groups in the community. Respondents noted that they had help with volunteers, equipment, putting together teams, coaching, entering tournaments and funding applications. Despite there being a perceived difference in approach by FC United and other 'bigger' clubs working in the area (that for instance FC are more inclusive than other clubs) respondents in the focus groups didn't feel that this detracted from the professionalism of the approach, something generally expected more from bigger clubs.

12. Focus Group Findings 2: Organisation

Most participants commented on the fact that they liked being involved with a football club, so football was seen to be a trusted vehicle for community working (more so than statutory providers, which may carry a level of social stigma) and that this extends into a pride in wearing the club badge/tracksuits. This was viewed by some as a positive social signifier ('when I walk down the street people can see I'm doing something with my life'), further underlining that football clubs can be a positive organisation for young people to coalesce around, particularly for groups who want to create socially cohesive projects.

There were some limitations identified with FC United's community engagement, as is perhaps to be expected with a relatively new organisation and one which is first and foremost a football club. Noted areas for improvement were a need for organised transport for participants, the availability of community officers and reliable communications; this is a particular issue when both FC and the partner organisations are voluntary and/or part-time, making it difficult to organise quickly. Some respondents also noted that volunteer roles could be unclear in terms of responsibilities and status. In light if some of these issues, FC has introduced a new Youth Forum, which is a pro-active attempt to improve communication and develop 'best practice'.

13. Volunteering the Political

It is clear that FC United has become established as a trusted volunteer-based community provider, as evidenced by the overwhelmingly positive feedback from participants and partner organisations. The plans for the Moston stadium reflect progress and promises further growth in terms of providing community assets and resources, notably for the local neighbourhood community. However, FC also represents the 'political' position(s) of its core supporter community (the owner-members) and there is a risk that FC's role in community provision, particularly if that is extended further into tendering for contracts for local services from existing public providers, may ultimately serve a conflicting ideological position to that of the core political values of the club. This conflict has yet to fully emerge, and is further complicated by the supporter community of FC United being divided as to the political profile or meaning of the club. Despite being born of fan protest on the future ownership of the game, there is a constituency of supporters who have been more recently drawn to the club (on the basis of access, affordability, match day experience) or who 'just want to go to a football match' for whom the politics in the structure of the club is a distraction at best and at worst a discomforting and therefore inappropriate dynamic within the club.

14. Conclusions

In terms of drawing conclusions about the future role of football clubs like FC United in delivering local services, it is clear that there are significant advantages in being able to use football as a vehicle for community engagement. This research found that a willingness and ability for cultural identification is vital, and that engaging with football clubs therefore offers a very important social and cultural signal of 'inclusion'. FC United also has resources – human and capital – and has earned leverage with public institutions. However there are risks associated with extending the role further beyond supporting existing community engagement work, to the tendering for local public service contracts.

Firstly there is the question of balancing the interests of the different communities the club seeks to serve (fans, neighbourhood, communities of disadvantage). Secondly, the current political climate for the VCS, as articulated through the Big Society agenda, means that there is a risk of being 'swept along' as unwitting agents in delivering government targets or engaging with a government strategy which does not sit easily with the prevailing 'politics' of the club.

The debate about the political profile of the club is starting to emerge as the club develops and moves beyond its initial core support. FC United recognise they have a *'need to establish our moral and political purpose'* via *'a clearly defined and easily understandable strategic position'* (FC United General Manager, Andy Walsh) but that this will not be easy; an overt 'political' position could jeopardise funding, limit provision and the willingness of other partners to engage. Perhaps most significantly, can any such position be agreed upon by the various communities who have a stake in the club?

Notes

[1] Department for Communities and Local Government, *Localism Act* (London: Her Majesty's Stationery Office, 2011).

[2] Cabinet Office, 'Open Public Services White Paper' (London: Her Majesty's Stationery Office, 2011).

[3] Figures for members, season ticket holders and registered volunteers correct as of 30/05/12 (source: FC United of Manchester club office).

[4] The club sometimes plays home games at Stalybridge or other local grounds when Gigg Lane is unavailable.

[5] Individuals buy shares to a value they can afford; irrespective of the value of the shares held, the shareholders voting power remains the same – one owner-member, one vote.

[6] Future Jobs Fund – paid short-term apprenticeships established under the previous Labour government. The FJF programme has now been closed by the current government and replaced with more unpaid internships and apprenticeship schemes.

[7] Chris Porter, 'Manchester United, Global Capitalism and Local Resistance,' in *Belgeo* 2 (2008): 181-191.

[8] Adam Brown et al., *Football and its Communities: Final Report* (Manchester: The Football Foundation and Manchester Metropolitan University, 2006).
[9] David Conn, *The Football Business* (Edinburgh: Mainstream, 1997).
[10] Ibid.
[11] Brown et al., *Football and its Communities.*
[12] Gavin Mellor, 'The Janus-Faced Sport': English Football, Community and the Legacy of the "Third Way"', *Soccer & Society* 9, issue 3, (2008): 313-324.
[13] Manuel Castells, *End of Millennium* (Oxford: Blackwell, 2000); Fred Coalter, 'Leisure Studies, Leisure Policy and Social Citizenship: The Failure of Welfare or the Limits of Welfare?' *Leisure Studies* 17.4 (1998): 21-36; Allan Patmore, Foreward to *Sport and Social Exclusion*, ed. Michael F. Collins (London: Routledge, 2003); Tom Burden, 'Poverty,' in *Policy Responses to Social Exclusion: Towards Inclusion?* ed. Janie Percy-Smith (Buckingham: Open University Press, 2000).
[14] Jonathan Long and Peter Bramham, 'Joining up Policy Discourses and Fragmented Practices: The Precarious Contribution of Cultural Projects to Social Inclusion?' *Policy & Politics* 34, issue 1, (2006): 133-151.
[15] PAT 10 (Policy Action Team 10), *Arts and Sport: A Report to the Social Exclusion Unit* (London: DCMS, 1999).

Bibliography

Brown, Adam, Gavin Mellor, Tony Blackshaw, Tim Crabbe and Chris Stone. *Football and its Communities: Final Report*. Manchester: The Football Foundation and Manchester Metropolitan University, 2006.

Burden, Tom. 'Poverty.' In *Policy Responses to Social Exclusion: Towards Inclusion?* edited by Janie Percy-Smith. Buckingham: Open University Press, 2000.

Cabinet Office. 'Open Public Services White Paper'. London: Her Majesty's Stationery Office, 2011.

Castells, Manuel. *End of Millennium*. Oxford: Blackwell, 2000.

Coalter, Fred. 'Leisure Studies, Leisure Policy and Social Citizenship: The Failure of Welfare or the Limits of Welfare?' *Leisure Studies* 17.4 (1998): 21-36.

Conn, David. *The Football Business*. Edinburgh: Mainstream, 1997.

Department for Communities and Local Government. *Localism Act.* London: Her Majesty's Stationery Office, 2011.

Long, Jonathan and Peter Bramham. 'Joining up Policy Discourses and Fragmented Practices: The Precarious Contribution of Cultural Projects to Social Inclusion?' *Policy & Politics* 34, issue 1, (2006): 133-151.

Mellor, Gavin. 'The Janus-Faced Sport': English Football, community and the Legacy of the "Third Way".' *Soccer & Society* 9, issue 3, (2008): 313-324.

Patmore, Allan. 'Foreward to *Sport and Social Exclusion*, edited by Michael F. Collins. London: Routledge, 2003.

PAT 10 (Policy Action Team 10). *Arts and Sport: A Report to the Social Exclusion Unit.* London: DCMS, 1999.

Porter, Chris. 'Manchester United, Global Capitalism and Local Resistance.' *Belgeo* 2 (2008): 181-191.

Governing the Football Community Agenda

David Hindley

Abstract

In recent years there has been a noticeable 'turn to community'[1] with attention on the potential role of football clubs as community institutions and a deliverer of social policy and neighbourhood renewal. As such there is now widespread adoption of the word 'community' in official football discourse[2] manifest in the Premier League's *Creating Chances* programme, and promoted by the Football League Trust, which was set up to oversee community and youth development activities at Football League clubs. This is a significant refocus from its antecedents in the late 1970s, when the Football in the Community initiative was established as a response to footballs problems, combating the spectre of hooliganism and improving fans' behaviour, rather than those of its communities. The new organisational structures of Football in the Community (FiTC) programmes raise interesting questions of governance and regulation. Financial and advisory support for community departments is now explicitly linked to the clubs implementing prescribed standards. This chapter aims to question how the football community agenda is being governed. It will focus on the complex interplay of a diverse range of policy actors and partnerships involved. It will also examine the shift towards community departments actively seeking independence from their host clubs, most commonly by adopting charitable status, and whether this has led to a dislocation of football clubs from their social responsibilities.

Key Words: Community, corporate social responsibility, governance, social inclusion.

*****

1. Existing Research

Concerns about the game's 'new commercialism'[3] and the increased public scrutiny of football's governance have spurred 'significant questions about the legitimacy of football clubs and their position in society.'[4] This leads the authors to suggest that in response, football clubs are looking to engage with their local communities and greater social disclosure. This has been manifest in recent regulatory debates in the football industry, and has led to growing evidence that the term 'community' is being mobilised by the game's governing bodies. Richard Scudamore, Chief Executive of the Premier League, claims 'community engagement is now woven into the fabric of football.'[5] Despite these platitudes, coloured by increased expectations on football clubs to work with groups and individuals with multiple needs and exclusions, Boyle presents a contrasting view, asserting:

football's core business doesn't encompass community engagement (...) it's not enough to say "we do football" – if you take the name of your community and trade on that, you need to give back something more.[6]

In addition to such scepticism, the process for achieving a social return from sport remains unclear, whilst the ways in which 'community' has been mobilised within the football industry raises interesting debates surrounding governance and regulation. As Brown et al. observe, 'there has been little strategic thinking from government, sport or football's governing bodies on how the game as a whole or individual clubs should organise responses to these policy agendas.'[7]

Existing research on football in the community has to date tended to pursue a two-pronged approach, concentrating on the organisational structure and operation of individual schemes[8] and more recently focusing on the need for more rigorous evaluations of football-based social inclusion projects.[9] While these issues are important, the governance of football's role in the community has often been overlooked, along with confusion about whose football clubs' communities and their responsibilities are. Hence, this chapter aims to advance the understanding of 'community' in the context of English professional football. It will then focus on how the new community football agenda is being governed, exploring the complex interplay of a diverse range of policy actors and partnerships.

2. Conceptualising 'Community'

Under New Labour there has been a 'turn to community'[10] as the preferred mode of governance in urban regeneration, with attention on building inclusive or mixed communities at the neighbourhood level. This has been repackaged as 'Big Society' under the new Conservative-Liberal Democrat coalition government. The term community has thus become shorthand for a means by which a wide range of desirable social outcomes can be reached,[11] leading Smith et al.[12] to assert that the communities discourse has been closely aligned with the policy focus on social exclusion.

Despite its enduring appeal and malleability there remains a danger of community becoming a meaningless, hollow concept. The term has reached 'buzzword' status, and has been overused within policy documents and public statements by politicians and policy makers. As Cochrane argues, community is often used 'as if it were an aerosol can, to be sprayed on to any social programme, giving it a more progressive and social cachet.'[13]

The notion of community is heavily contested. Despite its ubiquity, there is no single, accepted and generalisable definition as to what constitutes a community. Rather what emerges from the literature is an indistinct, umbrella term. Nevertheless, community remains a pervasive and attractive term. Hillery recorded

94 definitions of community, which helps to illustrate both the lack of clarity and amount of confusion surrounding the term's meaning.[14]

Given the contested nature of the term community it is unsurprising that in the context of football 'the meaning attached to the *community* label (…) has been, and continues to be, quite a large variable.'[15] Wagg similarly notes that there has been little formal evaluation of the term and its relationship with football,[16] while Brown et al. stress that 'just because the word 'community' has been attached to it, one can forgive football clubs for not having particularly clear ideas of who their communities are and how they should respond to them.'[17] Bale identifies a twofold conceptualisation.[18] The first is the community in which the club is located, after which it is invariably named, and which the club can be said to 'represent'. The second community is smaller, made up of the people and businesses lying in close proximity to the football stadium. Morrow meanwhile purports that a football club's community is made up of two interrelated and often overlapping dimensions: first, a 'direct' or 'traditional' community of supporters, and second, a wider notion that includes people and groups who can be affected either directly or indirectly by the existence and operation of a football club. What emerges from this discussion is that there needs to be a much more sophisticated and dynamic understanding of community.[19] As Brown et al. note, part of the difficulty stems from social change, which has led to re-constituted allegiances of class and kinship and in the geographical location of communities. In addition, the notion of community has been distorted and undermined because it has been 'sprayed on' to all manner of initiatives to indicate feelings of inclusiveness and tackling social deprivation.[20] There is no such thing as 'the community' as a homogenous entity, rather there are multiple – sometimes overlapping – communities, which exist beyond geography and encompass a wide range of social ties and common interests.

3. Community in a Sporting Context

The malleability of community has led to its usage in a range of contexts. The field of sport is no different in this regard, promoted as a potential instrument in the pursuit of diverse social policy agendas including enhancing health, engaging disaffected youth, combating anti-social behaviour, and helping to build stronger and safer communities.[21]

Football represents an attractive terrain for delivering the government's wider social outcomes due to its widespread popularity both at the elite level and at the 'grassroots'. Thus, football is increasingly regarded as one of the principal national institutions that reproduce desired core values, crucially however without actually questioning *whose* values football should be expected to promote.

The notion of football clubs as 'community' institutions is not a new phenomenon. For more than a century professional football clubs in towns and cities across England have been recognised as playing a key role in their local communities, helping to reinforce a sense of place and local identity.[22] During the late Victorian and Edwardian era many clubs were consciously established as sporting and community entities by churches, benevolent organisations and enlightened employers, commonly as focal points for the fostering of community. The labelling of football clubs as 'community' institutions meanwhile is probably most commonly understood as having taken place under the banner of the national *Football in the Community* (FiTC) initiative. The latter has its antecedents in the late 1970s when the Sports Council encouraged football clubs to combat the spectre of hooliganism by establishing formal schemes with the intention of attracting supporters and improving fans' behaviour. Notably the scheme was launched principally in response to football's problems rather than those of its communities.[23] By the early 1990s the FiTC initiative had become country-wide, helped by additional funding from the FA and the Football League, with many clubs now having independent community organisations operating as charitable bodies. Back et al. note that Football in the Community schemes act as a 'buffer' between clubs, the wider community and the issue of racial equality, going on to praise the progressive work of such initiatives 'while the inner workings of the football club remain unchallenged and unchanged.'[24] This view was reflected by the Football Task Force's 1999 *Investing in the Community* report[25] which whilst identifying pockets of good practice, expressed concerns about the coherence of FiTC programmes and the linkages with their local communities. Added to this, outside of the specific interventions of community programmes, is a relative lack of evidence to support arguments that football clubs as a whole are of value to their local communities in which they are situated and of the impact of clubs in a more holistic manner.

4. Research Design

Research for this article passed through a number of phases, beginning with an initial trawl of existing literature and research, before interrogating the annual reports of the governing bodies and agencies involved. These helped to provide a strong theoretical foundation, identifying key themes and establishing the lines of questioning for the empirical data collection. The findings presented below principally come from two semi-structured interviews, both of which were designed to offer critical insights into how football's role in the community is governed. The interviews were conducted with a senior representative from the Premier League, Simon Morgan (Head of Community Development), and Guy Rippon, one of the Football League Trust's Community Officers.

The interview content was then tabulated against these themes and analysed against the key research questions of the chapter. This information was then supplemented by detailed documentary analysis which focused on the current sporting and political contexts in which football clubs are increasingly expected to engage with new social agendas.

5. Findings

As noted, it is now commonplace for clubs to have designated community departments which are primarily involved in the delivery of community-based initiatives, whilst other areas of the club are responsible for dealing with 'customers.'[26] Indeed in recent years a number of community departments have sought independence from their host clubs, most commonly by adopting charitable status. Mellor suggests there are a number of benefits of such a strategy, citing a level of autonomy will enable clubs to overcome some of the potential tensions between commercial and community motivations. Conversely, by talking of business and community as if they were two separate things there is a danger this may (un)intentionally be promoting the idea that they involve discrete thought processes and activities.

What emerges from this is the importance of the football club's 'buy-in' to the community agenda as a crucial ingredient. As Taylor observes, 'despite the good intentions of the external agencies, there are still grounds for inferring that, left to their own devices, football clubs would take very little interest in putting themselves out for their communities.'[27] This sentiment is supported by Watson who observes 'we could achieve so much with the real commitment from the glamour clubs. But they're not interested.'[28] These vignettes suggest that there is great variability in the quality and scope of football community programmes, as well as differing experiences of those responsible with running such schemes and the relationship with their football club.[29] This may go some way to explaining the growing involvement of the game's governing bodies in shaping the football community agenda.

As outlined previously, there have been more instrumental attempts to build beneficial relationships between clubs and communities. This started as a Sports Council led initiative in the 1970s, before being run via the FiTC schemes, funded by the Footballers' Further Education and Voluntary Training Society (FFEVTS) to now the Football League Trust, Premier League and the Football Foundation. The latter was formed as a national charity in 2000, in which the Premier League was committed to allocating 5% of its television broadcasting deal, matched by the Football Association and the Government (totalling £135 million from 2009 to 2012) with a bold mission to improve grassroots facilities, create opportunities, and build communities. The funding arrangements are complex and cumbersome, comprising multiple layers and directions in which the finances travel. As Morgan explains:

> At the moment we have got a financial arrangement so that a percentage is ring-fenced and goes towards a combined community pot, so that money is then given back as part of the Premier League/PFA fund for Premier League clubs to access, and this sits within the Football Foundation. We also give the

Football League some money, which is overseen by the Football League Trust as a separate operation, and then there is the Premier League money which goes into the Football Foundation ... You can already see from this how piecemeal it is and that is just three organisations without thinking about the other organisations involved.[30]

Here Morgan alludes to the complexities of community development, which is 'cluttered and very piecemeal,' characterised by multiple stakeholders, policy actors and funding agencies. One of the challenges has been regarding the clear identification of roles and responsibilities, encapsulated by the Premier League's relationship with the Football Association:

They [the FA] are the governing body, whilst we [the Premier League] are the competition. At a professional level the clubs will deliver community work, an aspect of which is football development and by their very nature clubs have coaches so it is about aligning what our clubs are doing, and to avoid duplication.[31]

The Football League Trust is a charitable body established in 2007 to oversee youth and community development by the 72 clubs which make up the Football League. The Trust's community arm is charged with working with FiTC schemes 'to serve their communities and deliver four core themes: health, sports participation, social inclusion and community cohesion, and helping young people realise their potential.'[32] Rather than imposing uniform programmes upon its member clubs, the Trust has, through its regional managers, encouraged innovation under 'themed' priority areas of delivery and has invested heavily in building the capacity of clubs' community departments. As Rippon explains:

Trying to explain to people what our role is, is almost impossible because it change from one day to another. It is support, advice, guidance, help with accessing funding, a critical friend, and at the same point being a governance mechanism as well.[33]

The work with community schemes has caused challenges, as Morgan explains "some of the established FiTC schemes who didn't really have robust governance structures in place have basically had to start again from scratch (...) It is fair to say in the past they [the clubs] have been the delivery agents, it has all been about the delivery, whereas the need for management – the good governance – needs to go behind it.[34]

Rippon similarly observes that some Football in the Community programmes are moving more slowly than others with regards their level of professionalism. An additional hurdle to which Morgan alludes is the need for clubs to have in place more robust monitoring and evaluation, and thus move beyond the shortcomings of anecdotal evidence – 'All Premier League funding is attached to the need for monitoring and evaluation because without it we can shout about the power of football but we need proof behind that.'[35]

This reflects the view that while there are strong political claims that football can make a positive contribution to social issues, there is relatively little evidence to support these assumptions.[36] Interestingly, one consequence of this requirement for greater monitoring is a perception that this represents an additional layer of bureaucracy.

6. Concluding Remarks

The interview data serves to promote the contribution football can make to community regeneration, and that the game's authorities is playing a more significant and obvious role in supporting football clubs in delivering a range of social agendas. This has not been without its challenges – something perhaps not unexpected given the initial and in places continued scepticism towards football in the community programmes, and the fragmented and at times piecemeal nature of the partnerships and work in this area. Indeed two of the main themes to emerge are the need for greater strategic leadership and for greater consistency, again issues which could have been anticipated given the relatively infancy of the new governing arrangements.

What emerges is that the governance of the football community is inherently complex due to the diverse range of stakeholders and policy actors, as well as the political, cultural and structural nuances of the different organisations involved. Such a cluttered environment is characterised by multiple interests, and a complex combination of legal, regulated and self-regulatory frameworks. The involvement of the Premier League and the Football League Trust have both placed an emphasis on establishing a supportive framework and clear guidelines, designed to promote innovative practice and delivery at a local level which can be adapted to suit specific needs.

As this chapter has noted, while the establishment of independent community organisations has developed across the game, the recognition and incorporation of community interests within the core business of clubs has been far less extensive. This begs the question as to whether the football authorities should make more explicit the social expectations on their member clubs. By extending their role to promote and develop a more thorough and shared understanding of community engagement, and specifically the game's obligations and commitments to its communities, this would help to chip away at what Steve Waggott describes as 'vestiges of the old guard who question the motive of getting involved in community work.'[37]

Notes

[1] Robert Imrie and Mike Raco, 'Community and the Changing Nature of Urban Policy,' *Urban Renaissance? New Labour, Community and Urban Policy*, ed. Robert Imrie and Mike Raco (Bristol: Policy Press, 2003), 3-37.

[2] Stephen Wagg, ed., *British Football and Social Exclusion* (London: Routledge, 2004).

[3] Tom Cannon and Sean Hamil, 'Reforming Football's Boardrooms,' *Football in the Digital Age: Whose Game is it Anyway?* ed. Sean Hamil, Jonathan Michie, Christine Oughton and Steven Warby (Edinburgh: Mainstream, 2000).

[4] Richard Slack and Philip Shrives, 'Social Disclosure and Legitimacy in Premier League Football Clubs: The First Ten Years', *Journal of Applied Accounting Research* 9.1 (2008): 17-28.

[5] Adam Brown et al., *Football and its Communities: Final Report* (London: Football Foundation, 2006), 1.

[6] Dave Boyle, 'Football and Its Communities: Where Next?' Panel discussion at *Beyond Engagement: Inclusion, Sport and Popular Culture*, Substance conference, Manchester, 26-27 September 2007.

[7] Adam Brown et al., *Football and Its Communities*, 10.

[8] Neil Taylor, 'Giving Something Back: Can Football Clubs and Their Communities Co-Exist? *British Football and Social Exclusion*, ed. Stephen Wagg (London: Routledge, 2004); Sean Perkins, 'Exploring Future Relationships between Football Clubs and Local Government,' *The Future of Football: Challenges for the Twenty-First Century*, ed. Jon Garland and Dominic Malcolm, and Michael Rowe (London: Frank Cass, 2000); Neil Watson, 'Football in the Community: What's the Score?' *The Future of Football: Challenges for the Twenty-First Century*, ed. Jon Garland, Dominic Malcolm and Michael Rowe (London: Frank Cass, 2004).

[9] Richard Tacon, 'Football and Social Inclusion: Evaluating Social Policy,' *Managing Leisure* 12 (2007): 1-23.

[10] Robert Imrie, Loretta Lees and Mike Raco, eds., *Regenerating London: Governance, Sustainability, and Community in a Global City* (London: Routledge, 2009), 12.

[11] Victoria Nash and Ian Christie, *Making Sense of Community* (London: IPPR, 2003), 22.

[12] Ian Smith, Eileen Lepine and Marilyn Taylor, eds., *Disadvantaged by where You Live? Neighbourhood Governance in Contemporary Urban Policy* (Bristol: Policy Press, 2007).

[13] Allan Cochrane, 'Community Politics and Democracy', in *New Forms of Democracy*, ed. David Held and Christopher Pollitt (London: Sage, 1986), 51.

[14] George A. Hillary, cited in Sarah Banks, 'The Concept of Community Practice,' in *Managing Community Practice: Principles, Policies and Programmes*, ed. Sarah Banks, Hugh Butcher, Paul Henderson and Jim Robertson (Bristol: Policy Press, 2003), 13.

[15] Stephen Hope, 'Back to the Future? Fan Volunteering at Community Football Clubs,' *Voluntary Action* 6.3 (2004), 65-77.

[16] Stephen Wagg, ed., *British Football and Social Exclusion* (London: Routledge, 2004).

[17] Adam Brown et al., *Football and Its Communities*, 9.

[18] John Bale, 'The Changing Face of Football: Stadiums and Communities,' in *The Future of Football: Challenges for the Twenty-First Century*, ed. Jon Garland, Dominic Malcolm and Michael Rowe (London: Frank Cass, 2000).

[19] Stephen Morrow, *The New Business of Football: Accountability and Finance in Football* (Basingstoke: Palgrave, 1999).

[20] Adam Brown et al., *Football and its Communities: Final Report*, 9.

[21] Daniel Bloyce and Andy Smith. *Sport Policy and Development: An Introduction* (London: Routledge, 2010); Fred Coalter, 'Sports Clubs, Social Capital and Social Regeneration: "Ill-Defined Interventions with Hard to Follow Outcomes"?' *Sport in Society* 10.4 (2007): 537-559; Michael Frank Collins and Tess Kay, *Sport and Social Exclusion* (London: Routledge, 2003).

[22] John Bale, 'The Changing Face of Football: Stadiums and Communities', in *The Future of Football: Challenges for the Twenty-First Century*, ed. Jon Garland, Dominic Malcolm, and Michael Rowe (London: Frank Cass, 2000), 91-101.

[23] Coalter, 'Sports Clubs, Social Capital and Social Regeneration'.

[24] Les Back, Tim Crabbe and John Solomos, *The Changing Face of Football: Racism, Identity and Multi-Culture in the English Game* (Oxford: Berg, 2001), 183.

[25] Football Task Force, *Investing in the Community*, a submission by the Football Task Force to the Minister for Sport (London: Football Task Force, 1999).

[26] David Hindley, *'Playing the Game': The Application of Corporate Social Responsibility (CSR) in Professional Football.* (Milan: Universiti Bocconi, 2008); David Hindley, 'Wide of the Post: The Challenge of Corporate Social Responsibility in English Professional Football', Presentation at *2010 International Conference on Sport and Society*, University of British Columbia, Vancouver, Canada, 8-10 March 2010; Gavin Mellor, 'Mixed Motivations.'

[27] Taylor, *Giving Something Back,* 65.

[28] Cited in David Conn, *The Beautiful Game? Searching for the Soul of Football* (London: Yellow Jersey Press, 2004), 344-345.

[29] Hindley, 'Wide of the Post.'

[30] Interview, 7 May 2010.

[31] Gavin Mellor, 'Mixed Motivations: Why do Football Clubs do "Community" Work?', *Soccer Review 2005*, http://www.supporters-direct.org/docs/Soccer%20Review%202005.pdf#page=23.

[32] Interview with Guy Rippon, April 2010.

[33] Interview with Guy Rippon, 8 April 2010.

[34] Interview with Guy Rippon, 7 May 2010.

[35] Ibid.

[36] Richard Tacon, 'Football and Social Inclusion: Evaluating Social Policy,' *Managing Leisure* 12 (2007): 1-23.

[37] Interview with Steve Waggott, then the Chief Executive of Charlton Athletic Football Club. February 2008.

Bibliography

Back, Les, Tim Crabbe and John Solomos. *The Changing Face of Football: Racism, Identity and Multi-Culture in the English Game*. Oxford: Berg, 2001.

Bale, John. 'The Changing Face of Football: Stadiums and Communities'. *The Future of Football: Challenges for the Twenty-First* Century, edited by Jon Garland and Dominic Malcolm, and Michael Rowe. London: Frank Cass, 2000.

Banks, Sarah. 'The Concept of Community Practice'. *Managing Community Practice: Principles, Policies and Programmes*, edited by Sarah Banks, Hugh Butcher, Paul Henderson and Jim Robertson. Bristol: Policy Press, 2003.

Bauman, Zygmunt. *Community: Seeking Safety in an Insecure World*. Cambridge: Polity, 2001.

Bloyce, Daniel and Andy Smith. *Sport Policy and Development: An Introduction*. London: Routledge, 2010.

Boyle, Dave. 'Football and Its Communities: Where Next?' Panel discussion at *Beyond Engagement: Inclusion, Sport and Popular Culture*. Substance conference, Manchester, 26-27 September 2007.

Brown, Adam, Tim Crabbe, Gavin Mellor, Tony Blackshaw, and Chris Stone. *Football and its Communities: Final Report*. London: Football Foundation, 2006.

Brown, Adam, Tim Crabbe and Gavin Mellor, eds. *Football and the Community in the Global Context: Studies in Theory and Practice*. London: Routledge, 2009.

Cannon, Tom and Sean Hamil. 'Reforming Football's Boardrooms.' *Football in the Digital Age: Whose Game is it Anyway*, edited by Sean Hamil, Jonathan Michie, Christine Oughton, Steven Warby. Edinburgh: Mainstream, 2000.

Coalter, Fred. *A Wider Social Role for Sport: Who's Keeping the Score?* London: Routledge, 2007.

Coalter, Fred. 'Sports Clubs, Social Capital and Social Regeneration: "Ill-Defined Interventions with Hard to Follow Outcomes"?' *Sport in Society* 10.4 (2007): 537-559.

Cochrane, Allan. 'The New Urban Policy: Towards Empowerment or Incorporation? The Practice of Urban Policy'. *Urban Renaissance? New Labour, Community and Urban Policy*, edited by Robert Imrie and Mike Raco. Bristol: Policy Press, 2003.

Collins, Michael, and Tess Kay. *Sport and Social Exclusion*. London: Routledge, 2003.

Conn, David. *The Beautiful Game? Searching for the Soul of Football*. London: Yellow Jersey Press, 2004.

Conn, David. 'The People's Game'. *The Guardian*, 23 February, 2005.

———. 'Community Goals'. *The Guardian*, 9 August, 2006.

Dyreson, Mark. 'Maybe it's Better to Bowl Alone: Sport, Community and Democracy in American Thought.' *Culture, Sport, Society* 4.1 (2001): 19-30.

Etzioni, Amitai. *The Spirit of Community*. London: Fontana Press, 1995.

Football Foundation. *Community Programme: Strategy 2008*. 2008.

Football Task Force. *Investing in the Community*. A submission by the Football Task Force to the Minister for Sport. London: Football Task Force, 1999, http://webarchive.nationalarchives.gov.uk/+/http://www.culture.gov.uk/images/pub lications/investinginthecommunity.PDF.

Giulianotti, Richard. *Football: A Sociology of the Global Game*. Cambridge: Polity Press, 1999.

Hamil, Sean, Jonathan Michie, Christine Oughton and Steven Warby, eds. *Football in the Digital Age: Whose Game is it Anyway?* Edinburgh: Mainstream, 2000.

Haywood, Les, ed. *Sport in the Community. The Next Ten Years: Problems and Issues*. Ilkley: Leisure Studies Association, 1983.

Hindley, David. *'Playing the Game': The Application of Corporate Social Responsibility (CSR) in Professional Football*. Milan: Universiti Bocconi, 2008.

———. 'Wide of the Post: The Challenge of Corporate Social Responsibility in English Professional Football'. Presentation at *2010 International Conference on Sport and Society*, University of British Columbia, Vancouver, Canada, 8-10 March 2010.

Houlihan, Barrie and Anita White. *The Politics of Sports Development: Development of Sport or Development through Sport?* London: Routledge, 2002.

Hughson, John, David Inglis and Marcus Free. *The Uses of Sport: A Critical Study*. London: Routledge, 2005.

Imrie, Robert and Mike Raco. 'Community and the Changing Nature of Urban Policy'. *Urban Renaissance? New Labour, Community and Urban Policy*, edited by Robert Imrie and Mike Raco. Bristol: Policy Press, 2003.

Imrie, Robert, Loretta Lees and Mike Raco, eds., *Regenerating London: Governance, Sustainability, and Community in a Global City*. London: Routledge, 2009.

Ingham, Alan and Mary McDonald. 'Sport and Community/Communitas'. *Sporting Dystopias: The Making and Meaning of Urban Sport Cultures*, edited by Ralph Wilcox, David Andrews, Richard Irwin, and Robert Pitter. Albany, NY: State University of New York Press, 2003.

Long, Jonathan and Ian Sanderson. 'The Social Benefits of Sport: Where's the Proof?' *Sport in the City: The Role of Sport in Economic and Social Regeneration*, edited by in Chris Gratton and Ian P. Henry. London: Routledge, 2001.

McDonald, Deborah and Malcolm Tungatt. *Community Development and Sport*. London: Community Development Foundation, 1992.

Mellor, Gavin. 'Can we have Our Fans back Now? Football, Community and the Historical Struggles of Small-Town Clubs'. *Singer and Friedlander Football Review 2000/01 Season*, 2001. http://www.le.ac.uk/snccfr/resources/sf-review/00-01/01article7.html.

Mellor, Gavin. 'Mixed Motivations: Why do Football Clubs do "Community" Work?' *Soccer Review 2005*. http://www.supporters-direct.org/docs/Soccer%20Review%202005.pdf#page=23.

Mellor, Gavin. 'The Janus-Faced Sport': English Football, Community and the Legacy of the "Third Way".' *Soccer and Society* 9.3 (2008): 313-324.

Morrow, S. *The New Business of Football: Accountability and Finance in Football*. Basingstoke: Palgrave, 1999.

Mulgan, Geoff. *Living and Community*. London: Black Dog Publishing, 2008.

Perkins, Sean. 'Exploring Future Relationships between Football Clubs and Local Government.' *The Future of Football: Challenges for the Twenty-First Century*, edited by Jon Garland and Dominic Malcolm, and Michael Rowe. London: Frank Cass, 2000.

Raco, Mike. 'New Labour, Community and the Future of Britain's Urban Renaissance.' *Urban Renaissance? New Labour, Community and Urban Policy*, edited by in Robert Imrie and Mike Raco. Bristol: Policy Press, 2003.

Slack, Richard and Philip Shrives. 'Social Disclosure and Legitimacy in Premier League Football Clubs: The First Ten Years.' *Journal of Applied Accounting Research* 9.1 (2008): 17 - 28.

Smith, Ian, Eileen Lepine and Marilyn Taylor, eds. *Disadvantaged by where You Live? Neighbourhood Governance in Contemporary Urban Policy*. Bristol: Policy Press, 2007.

Smith, Jason M. and Alan G. Ingham. 'On the Waterfront: Retrospectives on the Relationship between Sport and Communities'. *Sociology of Sport* 20 (2003): 253-274.

Smith, M. K. 'Community'. In *Encyclopaedia of Informal Education*. 2001. http://www.infed.org/community/community.htm.

Tacon, Richard. 'Football and Social Inclusion: Evaluating Social Policy.' *Managing Leisure* 12 (2007): 1-23.

Taylor, Neil. '"Giving Something Back": Can Football Cubs and Their Communities Co-Exist?' In *British Football and Social Exclusion*, edited by Stephen Wagg. London: Routledge, 2004.

Wagg, Stephen, ed. *British Football and Social Exclusion*. London: Routledge, 2004.

Watson, Neil. 'Football in the Community: What's the Score?' In *The Future of Football: Challenges for the Twenty-First Century*, edited by Jon Garland and Dominic Malcolm, and Michael Rowe. London: Frank Cass, 2004.

The Nation's Game: Football and Nationalism in Spain

Lucía Payero López

Abstract

Football is the most popular sport in Spain. It reflects important aspects of society, so its study has considerable relevance for sociologists, anthropologists, historians, political theorists, and other scholars. Along these pages I want to focus on some political aspects involved in football. Particularly, I am going to highlight the connections between soccer and nationalism, trying to provide an explanation of those relations. To illustrate my point, the Spanish case will be useful, because national matters are one of the main political concerns within the country. Moreover, Spanish football provides good examples of how nationalism and sport are intertwined. The chapter is arranged in four parts. Each of them corresponds to one thesis which tries to develop more carefully my central view: the football field is particularly prone to national exhibitions, and they are uncritically accepted even by those people who do not call themselves nationalist, like most Spaniards.

Key Words: Football, nationalism, Spain.

*****

1

My first thesis has an empirical nature and it can be enunciated as follows: nationalism is widely rejected in Spain. Most Spaniards deny their nationalist affiliation, opting for alternative sources of political identity.[1]

Several reasons explain this spurning. First, the study of nationalism has been neglected, hence the lack of a serious scholarly debate on the matter.[2] In Spain the absence of a reliable nationalist theory contrasts with the political and social importance attached to the territorial model. As a result journalists and discussants on TV programmes create national identity, while self-styled scholars just sum up and gloss over those ideas born in the media. In this sense, an academic contemptuous attitude or, in MacCormick's words, *odium philosophicum* towards nationalism might seem less surprising:[3] the nation's ideology suffers from a 'philosophical poverty and even incoherence.'[4]

Second, nationalism is regarded as responsible for terrible crimes such as the Yugoslavian ethnic cleansing or ETA's terrorist attacks.[5] The nation's ideology is seen as a problem, and any government devotes considerable efforts and resources to combat it.

Third, as nationalism is philosophically inconsistent and morally despicable, most citizens and politicians in Spain say they are not nationalist, but constitutionalist. Moreover, the term nationalist specifically refers to the peripheral nations which lack a state.[6] According to Billig,

> Separatists are often to be found in the outer regions of states; the
> extremists lurk on the margins of political life in established
> democracies, usually shunned by the sensible politicians of the
> centre.[7]

This opposition between constitutionalists and nationalists relies on the
distinction between cultural and political nations, which requires further
explanation.

Modernist theoreticians of nationalism hold that every nation is produced,
created or invented by its own nationalism, so nations are 'imagined communities'
that only differ in the 'style in which they are imagined.'[8] As a consequence, the
type of nation – ethnic/cultural or civic/political – will be known after analysing
the nationalist discourse: the nationalist speech gives the clue (performative
nationalism). In this sense, I will talk of an *ethnic nation* when the objective
paradigm of community building is used, relegating the group member's freedom
to a second place: the political power is organised on the basis of already existing
ties, such as a common language, religion or history. Quite the opposite, a *civic
nation* will be the one which highlights its members' will in order to belong to it.

However, in Spain this dichotomy has been interpreted in a quite different
fashion in order to support the Spanish national unity. During the constitutional
debates in 1978 it was necessary to organise the coexistence of several nations
within the same territory. While some parliamentarians were in favour of
conferring equal rights to all nations, searching for a kind of federalist formula for
the state, the majority of the House wanted to privilege the Spanish nation (the
hegemonic one), either suppressing any reference to the nations on the periphery,
or recognising them just as cultural entities. The last option was finally adopted in
the text, where the term 'nation' was allocated to Spain, being coined the word
'nationalities' to refer to stateless nations.

The theoretical foundation of this model was elaborated by distorting
Meinecke's *Cosmopolitanism and the National State*. To depict the emergence of
nationalist movements in Europe during the XIX and the early XX centuries,
Meinecke talked of political and cultural nations. Where a state already existed, the
political nation provided *ex post* the cohesion its members required, while if the
cultural community was previous, the political power would be later organised on
the basis of those objective ties which bind the people regardless of individual will
(language, ethnicity, geography, religion, history...). But the final aim is the nation-
state in both cases.[9] Spanish interpreters of Meinecke, however, under the
influence of Hegelian distinction between 'people' and 'nation', read that a
political nation had a state, while a cultural nation neither possessed a state nor was
able to ever achieve it. Thus peripheral nations were denied self-determination
rights. Whether they are called 'nations' or 'nationalities', their nature is cultural.
As it has been previously pointed out, cultural and political categories make sense

when they are referred to the nationalist speech, but not to the state machinery: so it is inadmissible to use the state absence or presence as the key delimiting factor.

Such insistence on describing peripheral nations with cultural attributes and nation-states with political features is intended to legitimise state nationalism. Thereby, Spain would not only beat Catalonia or the Basque Country thanks to its greater brute force, but to its stronger moral standards as well: Spanish patriotism[10] would mean compliance with the values of democracy and human rights enshrined in the Constitution, while Catalan or Basque nationalism, which disapproves certain articles of the Constitution, would amount to totalitarianism and ethnic essentialism. I agree with the correspondence between political communities and democratic principles only under the premises of performative nationalism. A state can be antidemocratic, so its sole existence does not guarantee a civic idea of nation. Similarly, a stateless nation is able to stress the people's will in order to belong to it, matching the subjective paradigm of nation-building.

2

My second thesis is aimed to denounce a popular misconception which has been successfully instilled in people's minds by the Spanish intelligentsia: this fallacy consists in denying Spanish nationalism and calling its advocates *constitutionalists*. On the contrary, I argue that Spanish nationalism does exist, and it is even more powerful than its competitors.[11]

The second article of the Constitution says,

> The Constitution is based on the indissoluble unity of the Spanish Nation, the common and indivisible homeland of all Spaniards; it recognises and guarantees the right to self-government of the nationalities and regions of which it is composed and the solidarity among them all.

After reading this section three things must be concluded. First, the Spanish Constitution is nationalist. Constitutionalism serves to disguise Spanish nationalism, so constitutionalists are nationalists who devote their affection to Spain. Under this new perspective, constitutionalists cannot reject nationalism *in limine*, on pain of self-contradiction. Second, Spain is a cultural nation whose objective element of cohesion is history. The second article states that there is a reality prior to the Constitution which is, at the same time, its foundation: the Spanish nation. Third, the right of self-determination is forbidden to any people, but the Spanish one, an additional argument to conclude the ethnic nature of Spanish nationalism.

The seeming weakness of Spanish nationalism which several scholars reveal is explained by turning to Billig's banal nationalism. Billig has applied the term *banal nationalism* to 'the ideological habits which enable the established nations' –

those which own their own state – 'of the West to be reproduced.'[12] In this sense, nation-states are 'indicated, or *flagged*, in the lives of its citizenry' every day;[13] yet their nationalism becomes overlooked, because nationalist ideology is seen 'as the property of others, not of *us*.'[14] In Billig's words, 'the citizenry are daily reminded of their national place in a world of nations,'[15] but this reminder or *flagging* takes place so often that it is a 'familiar part of the social environment:'[16] it operates 'mindlessly, rather than mindfully.'[17]

In my opinion, state nationalism enjoys excellent health as its everyday representation shows. Only an expert eye is able to notice Spanish national reproductions because their constant presence renders them unnoticed and, in any case, innocuous.[18] As Billig has indicated, in established nations 'the community and its place are not so much imagined' – in Anderson's sense – 'but their absence becomes unimaginable.'[19] Moreover, 'if all the unwaved flags which decorate the familiar environment were to be removed, they would suddenly be noticed.'[20]

Moving slightly on, I would add that state nationalism remains unnoticed while its hegemony is beyond question. However, whether any aspiring nation endangers its superiority, banal nationalism will become *hot*, showing its teeth and fighting to maintain its line.[21]

Additionally, in Spain regional teams cannot play in official competitions, unlike in the United Kingdom, so they are not able either to defeat Spain – imagine the reactions after a Basque victory over the Spanish squad – or to win prestigious contests – regional teams are only allowed to take part in friendly matches. The government's stand is that the only accredited representative of the country is the Spanish squad. Furthermore, playing in the Spanish team is compulsory for any sportsman or sportswoman who is summoned by the national coach, as the article 47.1 of the Law of Sport lies down.[22]

3

My third thesis states that mass sport, particularly football,[23] constitutes a field especially prone to nationalist expressions. In MacClancy's words, 'sports (...) help to define moral and political community.'[24] 'The ability of sport to assist in the creation of a sense of identity (...) occurs' not less 'at the level of the nation-state'[25] than in the case of aspiring nations.

In the soccer sphere, teams represent the imagined community; they are a symbol of the nation. This is obvious when talking of the national team –Spanish squad embodies Spain, while the Catalan squad epitomises Catalonia–, but also occurs with private clubs: as a general basis, Basque teams represent the Basque nation, Fútbol Club Barcelona stands for Catalonia and Real Madrid symbolises Spanish people.

Here are a few examples which prove my point. Athletic Club of Bilbao's history is intimately linked to Basque nationalism, as the policy of *la cantera* (the youth academy) shows.[26] Many players, managers, presidents and supporters of the team have taken part actively in campaigns in favour of Basque independence from the times of the II Republic (1931-1936) until the present. One of the most politically conscious footballers was the goal-keeper José Ángel Iribar. In September 1975, less than two months before Franco's death, he and his fellow members of the Athletic wore black armbands during the game which followed the execution of two members of ETA and three members of FRAP (a Marxist revolutionary organization). Then, in 1976, he refused to play the significant 50th match for the Spanish squad, though having been invited to, and that gesture won him boos in away meets outside the Basque country. Recently, Athletic footballers, some of them as well-known as Joseba Etxeberria or Julen Guerrero, have supported several campaigns in favour of Basque national teams.

From its foundation, Fútbol Club Barcelona has been the Catalan team, conflicting with two Spanish-national sides: Real Club Deportivo Español,[27] based in Barcelona, and Real Madrid. Despite the different economic policy,[28] footballers and management of Barça have equally supported Catalan nationalism countless times. During the dictatorship, the club promoted Catalan folklore and culture,[29] offering what Nicolau Casaus has called 'passive resistance against a totalitarian regime.'[30] In Manuel Vázquez Montalbán's opinion, 'Fútbol Club Barcelona played the role of the army which Catalonia never possessed.'[31] In the Transition, politics became often intermingled with football: the two presidents of the Catalan regional government, Josep Tarradellas and Jordi Pujol, were often seen in the Camp Nou;[32] nationalist political meetings were held in the Palau Blaugrana;[33] and the president of the team, Agustí Montal, called for the restoration of both the Autonomous Statute, which had been passed in 1932 during the Republic, and the Generalitat of Catalonia (the Catalan government) in one of the annual meetings of the club. In 2005, players and management of Barça[34] supported a publicity campaign for Catalan national teams which was run by the Plataforma Pro Seleccions Esportives de Catalunya.

Real Madrid, for its part, has traditionally embodied the Spanish nation. Nobody could have explained it better but Raimundo Saporta, a prominent member of the club's management for more than 30 years:

> Real Madrid is and has been apolitical. It has always had so much influence because of its working for the State. At the time of its foundation in 1902, Real Madrid obeyed Alfonso XIII; in 1931, the Republic, in 1939, General Franco; and nowadays, it obeys His Majesty Juan Carlos. It is a disciplined club which loyally adheres to the governing institution of the nation.[35]

I only disagree with his depiction of that behaviour as non-political: loyalty to power represents a political attitude. Franco, supporter of Real Madrid himself,[36] exploited its good results to improve Spain's perception abroad.[37] With the then president's acquiescence, the legendary Santiago Bernabéu, the team became an unofficial ambassador of the regime. It can be arguable whether Real Madrid was prouder of improving the image either of Spain[38] or of Francoism (as Shaw[39] and MacClancy[40] seem to suggest), but in fact the team fulfilled both functions. The main reason why Real Madrid became the regime's representative was its sporting achievements, far more significant than the Spanish squad's accomplishments, and also than those of Barcelona and Athletic. Then, the side could be used as a national weapon against both internal and external *enemies*.

Perhaps the main characteristic of the history of Spanish football is the confrontation between Real Madrid and Fútbol Club Barcelona. This clash involves sports, nationalist and political aspects, which sometimes interweave. Particular significance acquired the signing of Alfredo Di Stefano, who having been drafted by Barcelona, finally played for Real Madrid owing to a FIFA's decision –under the influence of the Spanish representative in this organisation–. Supporters of Barcelona interpreted this measure as a governmental attack against their club's success because Di Stefano substantially contributed to the glory of Real Madrid, and consequently their feeling of being punished by a hostile nation grew.

Nowadays, the identification between Real Madrid and Spain still continues. In this sense, numerous Spanish flags – even pre-constitutional ones – can be seen whenever the team celebrates its victories at the Cibeles Fountain.

4

My last thesis is intended to highlight that national symbols are not regarded as aggressive or menacing at the football ground, even by those people who reject their nationalist affiliation.[41] Quite the opposite, nationalist expressions go unnoticed inside the stadium and sometimes they can be deemed a sign of civic-mindedness. Supposing a Spanish citizen does not wish Spain to win the World Cup, most of his fellow nationals will feel offended; furthermore, their rage will be increased if the *anti-Spanish* person decides to support any other squad, particularly the one which eliminates Spain. Such reaction is totally irrational and not founded on sports criteria: the Spanish team has recently started to win trophies, but the passion for *la Roja* (the Red) is very old. In fact, football fans are supposed to be good at suffering, which is considered a positive value, because unconditional supporting implies being with the team not just in health, but also in sickness.

Devotion to the nation does not stop at the level of the national squad, but reaches even further. In Spain whenever a particular club plays an international competition[42] against a foreign team, supporting the *Spanish* is expected, even when the representative of this country is the eternal rival in the Spanish League. For instance, if Real Madrid had played the final of the Champions League against Chelsea, fans of Barcelona should have wished good luck to Madrid's supporters or, at least, they should not have supported Chelsea publicly; and the other way round.

But why is nationalism not repelled in the sports arena, and acquires a different meaning? In my opinion, three reasons can explain it. The first one is related to the concept of banal nationalism. Football is one of those fields where the national flag is waved daily without arousing the slightest suspicion. In fact, citizens' uncritical acceptance of sports nationalism lies in its usualness.[43]

The second reason has to do with the role played by football as a safety valve of group tension. As Elias has pointed out, socialisation process implies self-controlling one's impulses, and that repression subjects the individual to great emotional stress.[44] In order to survive, society itself provides certain mechanisms to help people to release tension caused by overexerting in controlling their passions: one example is sport. In this sense, institutionalised football matches are means of relieving community's tension. On the one hand, football enables rivalry to be *peacefully* solved through the recreation of a symbolic battle: spectators are sure that both players and fans will escaped unhurt from the competition. On the other hand, in soccer games the participants can experience similar tensions to real life,[45] but with no risk. Such certainty in the harmlessness of the sports spectacle is essential to guarantee that spiritual peace and liberating catharsis will be brought after the victory, avoiding feelings of guilt with the opponent's defeat.

From my point of view, reasons one and two can explain why in Franco's era nationalist expressions on the football pitch were tolerated, although they were severely banned and punished outside the stadium: fans spoke Catalan, Basque or Galician, and waved outlawed flags.[46] According to Shaw, the authorities tolerated those national exhibitions on the understanding that a controlled relief of *deviated* nationalist passions was necessary[47] (reason two). However, I think that the regime chose the sports arena and not another public space because national demonstrations seem innocuous when they are associated to sport (reason one).

The third reason aimed at the above described identification between established nations and democracy, on the one hand, and stateless nations and exclusionary ethnicism, on the other. Supporting the Spanish squad constitutes a sign of public-spiritedness, while the opposite is considered provocative or even aggressive: in Castoriadis' words, the imaginary institution of society is at stake.[48] Due to the enormous importance of sport as a vehicle for worshiping the nation,[49] in Spain physical education is included in the curriculum from 6 to 17 years old, and most children are also involved in after-school sports activities. Apart from the values inherent in sport,[50] doing it represents an outstanding social activity, especially for males: boys play football during the break at school and high-school, being excluded from the group if they show no talent for soccer.[51] As Dunning has put forward, sport contributes to project images of desirable masculinity, helping men to feel good as members of the community and to build loyalty to the group, which is regarded as a social virtue.[52] Most kids who used to play football on the playground will never become professional players, but they will probably remember with nostalgia the good time they had there. The identification with footballers –that is, young athletic attractive men who play skilfully the sport most citizens would like to have excelled at– is pretty easy. Footballers and their fans embody the imagined community, hence the acceptance of nationalism inside the stadium: national symbols look harmless on the pitch, where most of us want to be the player number twelve.[53]

Conclusions

There are important links between football and nationalism, and the analysis of the Spanish scenario is useful to understand them. First of all, nationalism implies negative values in Spain, being usually associated to Catalans or Basques, not to Spaniards. According to Billig, established nations are daily reproduced, but this *banal nationalism* remains hidden because their triumph renders waving their flag needless. Further, public expressions of state nationalism go unnoticed due to their usualness. Football is one of those fields where the nation is worshipped without arousing suspicion, particularly in the case of nation-states. Citizens are educated to release in the stadium those tensions caused by self-controlling their instincts – a key requirement of social life –, and also to identify with the nation that their admired players represent.

Notes

[1] For example, social democracy, the 15-M movement, environmentalism, feminism, or neoliberalism.

[2] 'Unlike most other isms, nationalism has never produced its own grand thinkers: no Hobbeses, Tocquevilles, Marxes, or Webers.' Benedict Anderson, *Imagined Communities: Reflections on the Origin and Spread of Nationalism* (3rd ed., London: Verso, 2003), 4.

[3] Neil MacCormick, '¿Es filosóficamente creíble el nacionalismo?,' *Anales de la Cátedra Francisco Suárez* 31 (1994): 70.

[4] Anderson, *Imagined Communities*, 4.

[5] Paraphrasing the beginning of the *Communist Manifesto*, Moulines says that the spectre of nationalism is haunting chancelleries, parliaments, newspapers, universities, and public opinion all over Europe. Carlos Ulises Moulines, 'Manifiesto nacionalista (o hasta separatista, si me apuran).' *Isegoría* 24 (2001): 25.

[6] Mainly, Catalonia, the Basque Country, and Galicia.

[7] Michael Billig, *Banal Nationalism* (London: Sage Publications, 1995), 5.

[8] Anderson, *Imagined Communities*, 6.

[9] Friedrich Meinecke, *Cosmopolitanism and the National State* (Princeton: Princeton University Press, 1970), 11.

[10] Notice that the term 'nationalism' is avoided when talking of Spain.

[11] The opposition between constitutionalists and nationalists is the outcome of the reception of Habermas' constitutional patriotism in Spain, a theory which was 'misused as part of a wide-ranging debate on regional autonomy'. Jan-Werner Müller, *Constitutional Patriotism* (Princeton: Princeton University Press, 2007), 44. Habermasian prestige led Spanish nationalists to identify themselves with the Constitution, a norm which embodied the principles of democracy and human rights; consequently, those who confronted any aspect of the norm, such as the national organisation, were regarded as enemies of the Constitution.

[12] Billig, *Banal Nationalism*, 6.

[13] Ibid.

[14] Ibid., 5.

[15] Ibid., 8.

[16] Ibid., 38.

[17] Ibid.

[18] The flag hanging on a public building, national emblems borne on coins and bank notes, and the organization of broadsheets separating national from international news are some examples of banal nationalism.

[19] Billig, *Banal Nationalism*, 77.

[20] Ibid., 40-41.

[21] The angry reaction of the Spanish government to the Republican anthem being played by mistake during the final of the Davis Cup in 2003 represents a good example of it, intimately connected to the topic of this chapter. More recently, at the final of the King's Cup of football in 2009, played by Athletic Club of Bilbao and Fútbol Club Barcelona (Barcelona Football Club), both the king and the national anthem were booed; TVE1, the public channel, did not broadcast live during those minutes, apparently by mistake, and the whistling was removed from the pictures shown at half-time. Such manoeuvre was widely understood as a kind of censorship to protect the monarchy, one of the symbols of the Spanish nation, against a Basque-Catalan nationalist attack. This year the final of the King's Cup took place at Vicente Calderón stadium (Atlético of Madrid's ground) and the two teams were Athletic and Barça again. Considering the likely possibility of a new booing to the prince –the king was not attending owing to health problems– and the anthem, Esperanza Aguirre, the president of the Autonomous Community of Madrid and a loyal advocate of the Spanish nation, had previously suggested playing the match behind closed doors. Finally, her advice was not followed, but TVE1 suppressed the whistling again.

[22] Ley 10/1990 del Deporte.

[23] Football is *el deporte rey* (the king of sports) in Spain.

[24] Jeremy MacClancy, 'Sport, Identity and Ethnicity,' in *Sport, Identity and Ethnicity*, ed. Jeremy MacClancy (Oxford: Berg, 1996), 2.

[25] Ibid., 12.

[26] *La cantera* is the rule which states that only Basque players –those born or brought up in any of the seven provinces which Euskalherria, the Basque Country, consists of– can be signed up.

[27] Royal Spanish Sports Club – the very name was seen as a provocation by *culé* fans, according to Shaw. Duncan Shaw, *Fútbol y franquismo* (Madrid: Alianza, 1987), 22.

[28] Barça did not commit itself to fostering the youth academy; it rather preferred to spend vast sums on international stars in order to emulate its eternal rival –Real Madrid–.

[29] Shaw, *Fútbol y franquismo*, 212.

[30] Ibid., 214.

[31] Ibid., 215.

[32] Camp Nou is the stadium of Barcelona Football Club.

[33] The Palau Blaugrana is the sports hall where Barça basketball, roller-hockey, handball and indoor-soccer teams play.

[34] Such as Oleguer Presas, Hristo Stoitchkov, Óscar García, Joan Laporta, and so on.

[35] Paul Preston, 'Prólogo,' in *Fútbol y franquismo*, ed. Duncan Shaw (Madrid: Alianza, 1987), 13.

[36] Shaw, *Fútbol y franquismo*, 50.

[37] Alex J. Botines, *La gran estafa del fútbol español* (Barcelona: Amaika, 1975), 71.

[38] Enrique Gil de la Vega, cited in Shaw, *Fútbol y franquismo*, 58.

[39] Shaw, *Fútbol y franquismo*, 59.

[40] Jeremy MacClancy, 'Nationalism at Play: The Basques of Vizcaya and Athletic Club de Bilbao,' in *Sport, Identity and Ethnicity*, ed. Jeremy MacClancy (Oxford: Berg, 1996), 192.

[41] For example, at international matches Spanish flags are waved and the national anthem is played; supporters of Barcelona carry *senyeras* (the Catalan flag), while fans of Basque clubs bear *ikurriñas* (the Basque flag).

[42] Such as the UEFA Champions League, the UEFA Europa League, the FIFA Club World Cup.

[43] Lucía Payero, 'La nación se la juega: relaciones entre el nacionalismo y el deporte en España,' *Ágora para la educación física y el deporte* 10 (2009).

[44] Norbert Elias, 'Introducción,' in *Deporte y ocio en el proceso de civilización*, ed. Norbert Elias and Eric Dunning (México D.F.: Fondo de Cultura Económica, 1992), 55.

[45] Feelings of danger, fear, joy, hatred, nervousness, ecstasy, rage, pain or deep sadness.

[46] *Senyeras*, *ikurriñas* and *estreleiras* (the Galician flag of the left-wing parties).

[47] Shaw, *Fútbol y franquismo*, 183-185.
[48] Cornelius Castoriadis, *The Imaginary Institution of Society* (Cambridge: Polity Press, 1987).
[49] Payero, 'Nación se la juega,' 110.
[50] Such as competitiveness, effort, sacrifice, teamwork, obedience, discipline, and fair-play.
[51] Payero, 'Nación se la juega,' 104-105.
[52] Eric Dunning, 'Lazos sociales y violencia en el deporte,' in *Deporte y ocio en el proceso de civilización*, ed. Norbert Elias and Eric Dunning (México D.F.: Fondo de Cultura Económica, 1992).
[53] Payero, 'Nación se la juega,' 105.

Bibliography

Anderson, Benedict. *Imagined Communities: Reflections on the Origin and Spread of Nationalism*. 3rd ed., London: Verso, 2006.

Billig, Michael. *Banal Nationalism*. London: Sage Publications, 1995.

Botines, Alex J. *La gran estafa del fútbol español*. Barcelona: Amaika, 1975.

Castoriadis, Cornelius. *The Imaginary Institution of Society*. Cambridge: Polity Press, 1987.

Dunning, Eric. 'Lazos sociales y violencia en el deporte.' In *Deporte y ocio en el proceso de civilización*, edited by Norbert Elias and Eric Dunning. México D.F.: Fondo de Cultura Económica, 1992.

Elias, Norbert. 'Introducción.' In *Deporte y ocio en el proceso de civilización*, edited by Norbert Elias and Eric Dunning. México D.F.: Fondo de Cultura Económica, 1992.

MacClancy, Jeremy. 'Sport, Identity and Ethnicity.' In *Sport, Identity and Ethnicity*, edited by Jeremy MacClancy, 1-20. Oxford: Berg, 1996.

———. 'Nationalism at Play: The Basques of Vizcaya and Athletic Club de Bilbao.' In *Sport, Identity and Ethnicity*, edited by Jeremy MacClancy, 181-199. Oxford: Berg, 1996.

MacCormick, Neil. '¿Es filosóficamente creíble el nacionalismo?.' *Anales de la Cátedra Francisco Suárez* 31 (1994): 61-72.

Meinecke, Friedrich. *Cosmopolitanism and the National State*. Princeton: Princeton University Press, 1970.

Moulines, C. Ulises. 'Manifiesto nacionalista (o hasta separatista, si me apuran).' *Isegoría* 24, 2001: 25-49.

Müller, Jan-Werner. *Constitutional Patriotism*. Princeton: Princeton University Press, 2007.

Payero, Lucía. 'La nación se la juega: relaciones entre el nacionalismo y el deporte en España.' *Ágora para la Educación Física y el Deporte* 10, 2009: 81-117.

Preston, Paul. 'Prólogo.' In *Fútbol y franquismo*, edited by Duncan Shaw, 11-15. Madrid: Alianza, 1987.

Shaw, Duncan. *Fútbol y franquismo*. Madrid: Alianza, 1987.

Competing for the Turf? A Gendered Exploration of Using Football Talk in a Mental Health Project

Helen Spandler, Alastair Roy and Mick McKeown

Abstract

Football is often viewed as a useful mechanism for engaging men in public health and welfare programmes. However, because of the gendered construction of football, and especially the on-going marginalisation of women in the sport, it is also important to explore how gender relations and identities are constructed in these initiatives. This chapter draws on our evaluation of a project which uses football venues and football metaphor to deliver a mental health programme targeting men. First, we identified some of the benefits of using football talk. For example, it provided a flexible therapeutic tool which helped men make sense of, and address, their mental health difficulties in a context and language they could understand and relate to. In the second half we present a preliminary analysis of the ways in which gender was constructed and performed in the project. On one level, the project seemed to offer a 'convergent space' of gender mutuality and inclusivity. However, we also noted ways in which dominant gender relations and identities were re-produced in ways which might limit the deeper and wider benefits of the project. We believe there is much potential in exploring and developing the use of football and football talk as a way to engage men in therapeutic conversations without reinforcing gendered assumptions. However, in order to realise this potential, initiatives like these need continued funding and support, as well as criticality.

Key Words: Football talk, gender relations, health, masculinity, space.

*****

1. Introduction

Men's health has recently become a top public health priority. Traditionally men have been seen as not looking after their own health, taking greater health risks, not accessing health services, especially health promotion, mental health services or psychotherapy.[1] As such they are often seen as at risk of developing serious mental health problems and have a higher risk of suicide. As a result, there have been recent attempts to engage men who are deemed 'hard to reach' or 'difficult to engage' in various health programmes.[2] As the national sport in England, football is seen as a potential vehicle to aid engagement, which is steeped in a variety of assumptions about men's interest in the game.[3] This chapter presents a preliminary analysis of a programme which uses 'football talk' to deliver a mental health programme targeting men[4] and is based on a forthcoming article in the *Journal of Sport and Social Issues*. The wider context of football frames both as an attractive tool within these programmes *and* a need for sensitivity around how gender is constructed and played out within them.

We argue that because football is a contested and gendered field, understanding the use of football to engage men requires a gendered approach to analysis which is thoroughly and consistently 'relational'. This means that gender is not a given but is constantly performed, negotiated and contested, in relation to men *and* women. This 'relational' approach to gender positions men and women's welfare as interrelated and interdependent i.e. they can't easily be separated.[5] Hence, putting aside financial, social and material gain,[6] it can be argued that dominant gender relations are ultimately detrimental to both women's and men's mental health.

Football has been seen as a key site where dominant gender relations are constructed, maintained and amplified (and sometimes resisted).[7] Some sports scholars suggest that the *mere presence* of women, lesbians or gay men within the game presents a unique threat to the maintenance of male hegemony on and off the football field. In *The Stronger Women Get, The More Men Love Football,*[8] Mariah Burton Nelson argued that the more women have progressed in society, and the more they have challenged sexism and traditional gender roles, the more important sport has become in bolstering male privilege. Sport becomes a site – a 'last bastion' even – where, in the context of challenges to male dominance and hegemony, men can still feel and express their superiority, *as men.* This is often achieved through sports talk. Indeed 'sports talk' has often been seen as a way in which gender privilege is created, maintained and reproduced:

> Men use sports talk to establish their niche in the gender hierarchy... When men talk sport it is a competitive conversation – competing with information to establish who is the most informed – a verbal one-upmanship. This establishes the hierarchy – the one with the most information usually wins the argument – and unity: "we are men, talking about men's interests".[9]

Indeed sports scholars such as David Nyland have analysed how things like 'sports talk' radio shows, have become an 'attractive venue for embattled white men seeking recreational repose and a nostalgic return to a pre-feminist ideal and thus operate to restore masculine hegemony'.[10] The Andy Gray and Richard Keys affair is interesting in this respect. Although they were publically dishonoured and sacked by Sky Sports in 2011 (for insulting comments about the presence of a female assistant referee at a premier league match), they were quickly re-absorbed into the field by being given a regular slot on 'Talk Sport' (a popular radio show aimed at, and presented by men, and known for its traditional views about sport and masculinity).

2. A Football and Mental Health Programme

It's a Goal! is a mental health project targeting men that uses football to engage people with mental health needs in a group based therapeutic programme. Instead of being about playing or watching football, it uses football as a metaphor and a way of structuring the programme to make it accessible, engaging and non-stigmatising. For this reason, it is delivered at football venues (rather than health settings); focuses on goal-setting, team work and confidence building; and participants are called 'players' (rather than 'clients') and facilitators are called 'coaches'.

The programme has been going for a number of years and has been positively evaluated.[11] Our evaluation of this pilot programme in the North West of England suggested a number of positive benefits for those who participated. For example, participants showed significant improvements in mental health using a modified validated well-being Scale.[12] In addition, qualitative feedback from players indicated high satisfaction with the project. Football venues provided an engaging setting, and the theme of football operated as a helpful framework for the programme. In particular, players positioned it to mainstream services – with its emphasis on mutual support, team work and football talk, rather than 'experts,' 'boundaries' and medicalised language. It also has had 'football related' benefits. For example, some players who were initially very depressed and isolated actually reported getting interested in football again, following their local team, and a minority even attended matches or started playing again.

Notwithstanding these positive findings, we want to look more critically at the idea of using football to engage men. In particular, as the projects are based around the idea of using 'football talk,' we are interested in what kinds of gendered spaces are created and what types of gendered identities and relationships are supported and inhibited. We present here a preliminary analysis of some of our qualitative data – focus group interviews with players.[13] All of the coaches in the programme were men and whilst most of the players were men and most of the groups were all male, some women are also accessed the programme, some of whom also took part in the focus groups. Therefore, it is also interesting to look at the presence and participation of women within the project.

3. Football Talk as Therapeutic

As was the intention of the programme, football talk appeared to provide an important vehicle for men to talk about their mental health difficulties. Football acted as an initial 'hook' to engage men and provided them with a 'way in', helping them to initiate conversations and establish connections with other players. This was often facilitated by expressing shared interest in football via the familiar territory of 'banter' and making humorous comments about the opposing teams and local rivals. Football is often described as a universal language and expressing ones allegiance to a team was a useful 'opening gambit' which made men feel at

ease and more comfortable and this, in turn, helped them to 'open up' and talk
about their vulnerabilities. As researchers, we witnessed this and, as football fans
ourselves, we actively took part in football banter as a way of easing the tension
and breaking the ice before (and sometimes during and after) the focus group
discussions.

Football talk was used in the programme as a means of 'translating' difficult
psycho-social issues into a language that men could more readily relate to. For
example, reflecting on the qualities of various football players and team positions
(such as goalkeepers, defenders, midfielders, and attacker) was used to identify
personal characteristics. At the same time as the pilot programme was running,
Gary Speed, the Welsh football international, committed suicide and this
unfortunate event provided a focus for the players around how they deal with their
own mental health issues and the potential consequences of not 'opening up' and
talking about their problems with others. It seemed that 'footy talk' operated as an
'intermediary language' allowing men to talk about their emotions and support
each other. Framing difficulties through football offered a medium which felt
familiar, acceptable and safe. In addition, talking about football also offered 'light
relief' when conversations got too 'heavy', painful or difficult.

4. Football Projects as Convergent Spaces

Football is often seen as inherently exclusionary, both in terms of the 'us and
them' of football rivalries and by excluding or marginalising certain groups (such
as women, lesbians and gay men).[14] Whilst none of the players 'came out' as
lesbian or gay in the interviews, some women did participate in the IAG!
programme, despite the fact that it targeted men. The women did not report being
put off by the football talk and banter and, notably, reported similar benefits to the
male players. Despite not identifying as football fans, the women (and indeed some
of the men who admitted not being fans) still felt that the football examples made
sense because of football's 'universal language'.

Whilst there was some disagreement amongst the male players about whether
groups should be mixed sex (i.e. include women) or be men-only, discussions
about this offered some interesting reflections. Most (but not all) of the male
players felt including women would be beneficial. Players who had been in the
programme with women reported how barriers were broken down between
different men and between men and women. For example, despite gender
stereotypes, men reported realising that 'women struggle with emotions too'; and
women could see that men could talk about their emotions. In these ways, these
football projects potentially operate as 'convergent spaces' emphasising a shared
humanity and bringing together convergent interests of men and women.[15] As
such, they may be important in helping to prefigure new forms of gender identity
and relationships, such as expressions of what has been termed 'inclusive
masculinity' (a normative form of masculinity based on gender inclusiveness).[16]

However, whilst clearly acknowledging the importance of football talk in providing a common language many men could relate to, the issue of inclusivity is more complex. The analysis so far relies on self-reports and whilst these are very important we also need to recognise the limitations of this approach. As stated, we only spoke to those who completed the programme, who are those most likely to have a positive experience. In addition, if we had conducted individual interviews it is possible that some people may have found space to be more critical. We only spoke to a small number of women and they were taking part in a group interview made up of a majority of men which may have influenced their responses.[17] In this context it is important not to just 'read off' what people say as if it represents reality in any simplistic way. Indeed our use of group interviews was interesting and worthwhile precisely because we could also make some observations about the dynamics in the group settings (which we expected would likely 'mirror' the dynamics at play during the programme).[18] Therefore, the following is based on some preliminary observations and reflections which revealed a complex picture of football projects as both 'convergent' and 'paradoxical' spaces which both challenge and reinforce dominant gender relations.

5. Football Projects as Reproducing Dominant Gender Relations

The women we spoke to did not appear to 'compete for the turf' in terms of football talk. They tended to emphasise how they weren't 'really' football fans and didn't know much about football. In some ways, the women kept themselves 'in their place' as self-identified 'girls' (despite their adult age), rather than knowledgeable football fans, or equals. We are not suggesting that the women were dishonest about their (lack of) interest in football. It is highly likely that they were not big football fans. However, it is also possible that downplaying an interest in football allowed them a more acceptable place within the group, one which didn't challenge their gendered status. In these ways they could be seen as displaying an 'emphasised femininity'.[19] This tended to reinforce a certain idea of the women's role in (i.e. outside/on the edges of) football. In other words, their presence didn't upset, subvert or challenge dominant gender relations. We might also tentatively suggest that not being 'real' football fans gave the small number of women attendees a more 'acceptable' (and non-threatening for the men) presence within the programme. Whilst this suggestion is speculative, it would be interesting to see how a woman would be received if she did 'compete for the turf'.

6. Football Talk as Performing Defensive Masculinity

The second issue we noted was the apparent (re) production of a particular gendered and heteronormative space within the group discussions. As has been argued elsewhere, although *direct* homophobia may have lessened in English society, it has been replaced by a more covert form of heteronormativity or heterosexism. This is often evidenced what has been called a 'defensive' masculinity or heterosexuality'. This relates to the way that men attempt to prove and reinforce their masculinity characterised by the 'expressive signalling of heterosexuality through a variety of repeated mechanisms'.[20] The men often emphasised their masculinity and heterosexuality (for example, by commenting on the potential sexual allure of women who may participate in the group) and asserted their essentialised difference from women, despite (or perhaps because of) the setting. This seemed to be particularly evident when dominant forms of masculinity appeared to be at risk (e.g. from too much disclosure or homosocial bonding). In turn, the women sometimes commented on the attractiveness of particular male professional football players which could be seen as another way in which they were able to play the (gender) game and be accepted (and acceptable) amongst the group. Whilst this dynamic may be a way in which many men and some women sought to feel comfortable and at ease, we noted that it also appeared to inadvertently exclude discussion of other important issues such as sexual abuse and sexuality. What is important here is that these issues have an impact on men's (and women's) mental health and these gendered dynamics operate to demarcate the bounds of acceptable territory for discussion.

7. Conclusion

In the context of health-related initiatives, sporting referents or metaphors appear to be a very intriguing and beneficial means of engaging some men (and women) in therapeutic conversations. Yet these football contexts can be seen as gendered spaces that have both 'inclusive' and 'defensive' elements.[21] Given the on-going marginalisation of women in football, the gender composition of such groups and the gender dynamics at play, seem to be important topics for on-going discussion and analysis. Indeed there was some evidence that reflecting on the situation of including women in the programme, could mirror wider changes happening in football and even anticipate or 'prefigure' future possibilities (e.g. the greater equality and participation of women, lesbians and gay men in football).[22]

Finally, it is important to recognise that the fragility of funding for these kinds of initiatives – especially in the current socio-economic climate – create pressures to 'succeed' (judged by metrics such as the numbers completing the programme). This might influence what conversations are encouraged or discouraged within the programme and result in conservative or defensive practice and a desire not to 'rock the boat' and keep everyone on board. It can also limit players making any critical reflections – especially to the 'evaluators' – because they generally value the programme and want it to continue.

It is clear that there is much potential in exploring, developing and expanding the use of football talk as a way to engage men in therapeutic conversations without reinforcing gendered assumptions. However, in order to realise this potential, initiatives like these need continued funding and support to fully develop. This seems to be the most urgent task.

Notes

[1] Damien Ridge, Carol Emslie and Alan White, 'Understanding how Men Experience, Express and Cope with Mental Distress: Where Next?' *Sociology of Health and Illness* 33.1 (2011): 145-59; Steve Robertson, 'If I let a goal in, I'll get beat up': Contradictions in Masculinity, Sport and Health, *Health Education Research* 18.6 (2003): 706-716.

[2] Alan White and Karl Witty, 'Men's Under-Use of Health Services: Finding Alternative Approaches', *Journal of Men's Health* 6.2 (2009): 95-97; Robertson, 'If I let a goal in, I'll get beat up', 706-716.

[3] Gerard Donaghy, 'The Crying Game,' *Mental Health Nursing* 26.2 (March 2006): 24; A. Jones. 'Football as a Metaphor: Learning to Cope with Life, Manage Emotional Illness and Maintain Health through to Recovery,' *Journal of Psychiatric and Mental Health Nursing* 16.5 (2009): 488-492; Alan Pringle and Pete Sayers, '"It's a Goal!" Basing a Community Psychiatric Nursing Service in a Local Football Stadium,' *Journal of the Royal Society for the Promotion of Health* 124 (2004): 234-238; Laura Steckley, 'Just a Game? The Therapeutic Potential of Football,' in *Facing Forward: Residential Child Care in the 21st Century*, ed. David Crimmens and Ian Milligan (Dorset: Russel House, 2005), 137-147.

[4] Helen Spandler and Mick McKeown, 'A Critical Exploration of Using Football in Health and Welfare Programs: Gender, Masculinities and Social Relations,' *Journal of Sport and Social Issue* 36.4 (2005): 387-409; Helen Spandler, Mick McKeown and Alastair Roy, *Evaluation of It's a Goal! Pilot Programme in North West England* (Preston: University of Central Lancashire, 2012).

[5] Dorothy H. Broom, 'Men's Health and Women's Health: Deadly Enemies or Strategic Allies?' *Critical Public Health* 19.3-4 (2009): 269-277; Alex Broom and Philip Tovey eds., *Men's Health: Body, Identity and Social Context* (London: John Wiley and Sons, 2009).

[6] These advantages have been referred to as a 'patriarchal dividend.' R. W. Connell and James W. Messerschmidt, 'Hegemonic Masculinity: Rethinking the Concept,' *Gender and Society* 19.6 (2005): 829-859.

[7] Lois Bryson, (1987) 'Sport and the Maintenance of Masculine Hegemony,' *Women's Studies International Forum* 10.4 (nd): 349-360.

[8] Burton Nelson is actually referring to American football but the argument could equally be made about any culturally dominant sport because the dominant sport in every country is male dominated and systematically excludes women.

[9] Mariah Burton Nelson, *The Stronger Women Get, the More Men Love Football: Sexism and the American Culture of Sports* (New York: Harcourt Brace, 1994).

[10] David Nylund, 'When in Rome: Heterosexism, Homophobia, and Sports Talk Radio,' *Journal of Sport and Social Issues* 28.2 (2004): 136-168.

[11] We evaluated the programme as a pilot programme which was delivered in 7 football clubs across the North West of England as a partnership between local

PCTs and football clubs. Pringle Sayers. '"It's a Goal!", 234-238; Alan Pringle and Pete Sayers, '"It's a Goal!" The Half Time Score,' *Mental Health Nursing* 26.3 (2006): 14-17; Mike Smith and Alan Pringle, *The Latest Score: An Evaluation of the It's a Goal Programme* (Nottingham: University of Nottingham, 2006). Spandler, Mckeowan and Roy, *Evaluation of It's a Goal!*

[12] The Warwick-Edinburgh Mental Well-Being Scale (WEMWBS). Ruth Tennant et al., 'The Warwick-Edinburgh Mental Well-Being Scale (WEMWBS): Development and UK Validation,' *Health and Quality of Life Outcomes* 5.63 (2007): 1-13.

[13] We conducted 6 group interviews which included a total of 40 players who had completed the IAG! programme (38 men and 2 women). This analysis is based on an early first stage analysis of talk relating to gender in the group interviews. We are currently conducting a fuller analysis of this data.

[14] Laura Kelly, 'Social Inclusion through Sports Based Interventions?' *Critical Social Policy* 31.1 (nd): 126-150. Robertson, 'If I let a goal in.'

[15] Helen Spandler, 'Spaces of Psychiatric Contention: A Case Study of a Therapeutic Community,' *Health and Place* 15.3 (2009): 841-847. Spandler and McKeown, 'A Critical Exploration.'

[16] Eric Anderson, 'Orthodox and Inclusive Masculinity: Competing Masculinities amongst Heterosexual Men in a Feminized Terrain,' *Sociological Perspectives* 48.3 (2005): 337-355.

[17] It is however, important to note the majority of the groups interviews were jointly facilitate by a woman and a male facilitator. We hope to look further into the possible implications of this in later work.

[18] For more exploration of the idea of 'parallel processes' in research see David N. Berg and Kenwyn K. Smith, eds., *Exploring Clinical Methods for Social Research* (London: Sage, 1985).

[19] Emphasised femininity, or what has been called an 'embodied femininity' of female football fans and players in Jayne Caudwell, 'Gender, Feminism and Football Studies,' *Soccer & Society* 12.3 (2011): 330-344.

[20] Anderson, 'Orthodox and Inclusive Masculinity,' 345.

[21] Despite recent attacks on the concept of 'hegemonic masculinity' we still think this Gramscian concept has currency because it helps us to understand the ways in which dominant masculinities can be challenged and can shift and change over time (cf. Connell and Messerschmidt, 'Hegemonic Masculinity,' 829-859). This means that whilst masculine hegemony is challenged it is also constantly reinventing itself. Thus even so-called 'inclusive' masculinity could become the new 'hegemonic' masculinity. New forms of masculinities, by demonstrating flexibility and hybridity, may make actually make male hegemony harder to challenge (see Demetrakis Z. Demetriou, 'Connells' Critique of Hegemonic Masculinity,' *Theory and Society* 30.3 (2001): 337-361). The Andy Gray and

Richard Keys affair is interesting in this respect. Their sacking by Sky Sports was not only ironic (they have such a poor track record of women's participation) it can also be seen as a process of demonstrating sport's (and masculinity's) reasonableness. Arguably, rather than undermining the dominant gender order, this strategy preserves the legitimacy of masculine hegemony and ensures its survival. [22] As we write this, we note the increased interest in women's football during the London Olympics 2012, especially given the success of the Women's Team GB and their manager, Hope Powell (a very successful black woman and 'out' lesbian).

Bibliography

Anderson, Eric. 'Orthodox and Inclusive Masculinity: Competing Masculinities amongst Heterosexual Men in a Feminized Terrain.' *Sociological Perspectives* 48.3 (2005): 337-355.

Berg, David N. and Kenwyn K. Smith, eds. *Exploring Clinical Methods for Social Research*. London: Sage, 1985.

Broom, Dorothy H. 'Men's Health and Women's Health: Deadly Enemies or Strategic Allies?' *Critical Public Health* 19.3-4 (2009): 269-277.

Broom, Alex and Philip Tovey, eds. *Men's Health: Body, Identity and Social Context*. London: John Wiley and Sons, 2009.

Bryson, Lois. 'Sport and the Maintenance of Masculine Hegemony.' *Women's Studies International Forum* 10.4 (1987): 349-360.

Burton Nelson, Mariah. *The Stronger Women Get, the More Men Love Football: Sexism and the American Culture of Sports*. New York: Harcourt Brace, 1994.

Caudwell, Jayne. 'Gender, Feminism and Football Studies.' *Soccer & Society*, 12.3 (2011): 330-344.

Connell, R. W. *Masculinities* (Cambridge: Polity Press, 1995).

———. 'On Hegemonic Masculinity and Violence: Response to Jefferson and Hall,' *Theoretical Criminology* 6.1 (2005): 89-99.

Connell, R. W. and James W. Messerschmidt, 'Hegemonic Masculinity: Rethinking the Concept.' *Gender and Society* 19.6 (2005): 829-859.

Demetriou, Demetrakis Z. 'Connells' Critique of Hegemonic Masculinity: A Critique.' *Theory and Society* 30.3 (2001): 337-361.

Donaghy, Gerard. 'The Crying Game.' *Mental Health Nursing* 26.2 (March 2006).

Jones, A. 'Football as a Metaphor: Learning to Cope with Life, Manage Emotional Illness and Maintain Health through to Recovery.' *Journal of Psychiatric and Mental Health Nursing* 16.5 (2009): 488-492.

Kelly, Laura. 'Social Inclusion through Sports Based Interventions?' *Critical Social Policy* 31.1 (2011): 126-150.

Nylund, David. 'When in Rome: Heterosexism, Homophobia, and Sports Talk Radio.' *Journal of Sport and Social Issues* 28.2 (2004): 136.

Pringle, Alan. 'Can Watching Football be a Component in Developing Good Mental Health in Men?' *Journal of the Royal Society for the Promotion of Health* 124.3 (2004): 124-128.

Pringle, Alan and Pete Sayers. '"It's a Goal!" The Half Time Score.' *Mental Health Nursing* 26.3 (2006): 14-17.

Pringle, Alan and Pete Sayers. '"It's a Goal!" Basing a Community Psychiatric Nursing Service in a Local Football Stadium,' *Journal of the Royal Society for the Promotion of Health* 124 (2004): 234-238.

Ridge Damien, Carol Emslie and Alan White. 'Understanding how Men Experience, Express and Cope with Mental Distress: Where Next?' *Sociology of Health and Illness* 33.1 (2011): 145-159.

Robertson, Steve. '"If I let a goal in, I'll get beat up": Contradictions in Masculinity, Sport and Health.' *Health Education Research* 18.6 (2003): 706-716.

————. *Understanding Men and Health: Masculinities, Identity and Well-Being.* Buckingham: Open University Press, 2007.

Rose, Gillian. *Feminism and Geography: The Limits of Geographical Knowledge.* University of Minneapolis: Minnesota Press 1993.

Smith, Mike and Alan Pringle. *The Latest Score: An Evaluation of the It's a Goal Programme.* Nottingham: University of Nottingham, 2010.

Spandler, Helen. 'Spaces of Psychiatric Contention: A Case Study of a Therapeutic Community.' *Health and Place* 15.3 (2009): 841-847.

Spandler, Helen, Mick McKeown and Alastair Roy. *Evaluation of It's a Goal! Pilot Programme in North West England.* Preston: University of Central Lancashire, 2012.

Spandler, Helen and Mick McKeown. 'A Critical Exploration of Using Football in Health and Welfare Programs: Gender, Masculinities and Social Relations.' *Journal of Sport and Social Issues* (forthcoming).

Steckley, Laura. 'Just a Game? The Therapeutic Potential of Football.' In *Facing Forward: Residential Child Care in the 21st Century*, edited by David Crimmens and Ian Milligan, 137-147. Lyme Regis: Russell House Publishing, 2005.

Tennant, Ruth, Louise Hiller, Ruth Fishwick, Stephen Platt, Stephen Joseph, Scott Weich, Jane Parkinson, Jenny Secker and Sarah Stewart-Brown. 'The Warwick-Edinburgh Mental Well-Being Scale (WEMWBS): Development and UK Validation.' *Health and Quality of Life Outcomes* 5.63 (2007): 1-13.

White, Alan and Karl Witty. 'Men's Under-Rse of Health Services: Finding Alternative Approaches.' *Journal of Men's Health* 6.2 (2009): 95-97.

The Gendered Significance of Community for Female Football Fans

Carrie Dunn

Abstract

This chapter examines the gendered significance of community for football fans. My research suggests there is a growing significance attached to supporters' involvement in the running of their club through the trust co-operative movement, offering a new way for supporters to become involved in the life of their club, and become part of a new, wider, national and international fan community, broader than simple club allegiance. This chapter relates these concepts to my qualitative interview findings, using case studies of respondents who are involved with the supporters' trust movement as part of their fandom. I suggest that female fans are particularly attracted to the democratic nature of supporters' trusts, and also examine exactly how and why respondents have become involved, looking at the 'gendering' of roles within the movement, and comparing their experiences as they have described them in interview.

Key Words: Community, fandom, female fans, gender, supporters' trust.

*****

1. Football and Community

In the UK, football clubs are generally owned by one rich individual or a consortium,[1] putting their own money in initially, then running it as a business intended to make profit. However, in recent years, as new stadia have been constructed, the financial situations of clubs altered due to accumulation of debt after the building process, and fans have become increasingly involved in encouraging clubs to stay rooted in their community. Since 1992, there have been over 40 cases of insolvency proceedings involving league clubs; it has frequently been the supporters who have rescued their club from administration, receivership or liquidation; for example, when Luton Town's new owner threatened to liquidate the club, it was a group of supporters who took on a debenture from a previous creditor, enabling them to call in the debt and seize control.

Supporters are now using their collective influence as a bargaining chip, seeking a voice in the community and in the running of their club, primarily through the supporters' trust cooperative movement, with over 110 trusts in England now owning shares in their clubs.

2. The Supporters' Trust Movement

A trust is a registered company, mostly set up as an industrial and provident society, where one share is owned by each member, and governed by an elected board. Money made is invested back into the organisation to further its aims and objectives; in practice, with supporters' trusts, this means buying shares in the club, or funding community projects.

There is also demand for supporter representation at director level; fundamentally, the sector's consumers want involvement in a company's board; rather than choosing to take their custom elsewhere, they seek change from within. Fans have the option of taking effective collective action if they disapprove of or disagree with the direction a club's ownership is taking.

3. The Appeal of the Supporters' Trust Movement to Female Football Fans

Received wisdom is that female fans are more likely to become involved in the trust movement than males. The then chief executive of Supporters Direct, Dave Boyle reported: 'In our experience, women have a higher representation within Trust membership, and within Trust activists, than the strict demographic proportion of women in a normal football crowd.'[2] Admittedly this is anecdotal evidence; however, 56% of my respondents supported a club with an active trust of which they were aware, and 62% of those respondents were members of the trust. In comparison, 89% supported a club that had a traditional supporters' club, but of those respondents only 38% of them were members.

The community ethos driving the trust movement offers a new way of supporting for those concerned with their club's position in the locality and the outreach work that can be done with marginalised groups. This concern to extend football to all interested parties – not just the traditional male, working/lower-middle-class demographic – may explain the attraction of the trust movement for female fans, and support Boyle's observation that more women than are proportional to the supporting demographic are involved in the movement.

A supporters' trust, though, needs to adhere to very strict rules to maintain its status as an Industrial and Provident Society: accounts need to be produced and audited; meetings must be minuted; elections must be held. If what Boyle says is true about women being attracted to the trust movement, it is possible that this is at least in part because of its democratic set-up, meaning that every member has a vote, rather than policy being decided by whoever is most vocal in their opinions. However, it is also possible that women then get drawn into working behind the scenes of the trust in an administrative or supportive role, rather than a more obvious or 'prestigious' spokesperson role. More practically, in general more women than men work part-time; according to the Equal Opportunities Commission, 82% of part-time workers are female,[3] so part-time working women – even though they may have additional domestic duties, including childcare – could be considered to have more spare time than full-time working men.

The next section looks at case studies of respondents' experience within the supporters' trust movement, comparing and contrasting narratives of fans from QPR and from Watford.

4. Tracy: QPR First

QPR First was formed in April 2001, following a public meeting at Hammersmith Town Hall. Tracy is one of the key figures, and she explains her initial involvement as partly because of her role as a mother, which means that she works part-time and gives her more free time to devote to other interests. She says:

> What happened was, I'd been reading the various things on different lists. The media at that time as well, there had been quite a bit about the setting up of Supporters Direct, which as you know comes out from the foundation. We were like, there was myself and a couple of others who were really keen on the idea. So what I did, because I'm local, well, local-ish in the London area, and because I work evenings, I was able to go to a couple of workshops and meetings that Supporters Direct were holding at that particular time to give advice and to help people and say look, this is what it's all about.

One possible interpretation of this narrative is that she is the person who actively wishes to 'give advice and to help people', and thus she is acknowledging her interest in the issues, which she flags up at the beginning of this extract by saying that she had been reading the coverage of Supporters Direct's foundation. However, I suggest a more likely interpretation would be SD are providing the advice, and she perceives her reasons for becoming involved in the first place in terms of her proximity (being 'local-ish' to London) and the free time that she has, rather than her own abilities and interest.

As her commitment has grown and deepened, she describes her reasons for staying involved in highly emotive, almost evangelical, terms, and remains committed and highly vocal about what the trust stands for, as she explains:

> It's been proved that we do need to know what's going on at our clubs. We nearly went out of existence because we didn't know what was going on. You still get people, oh supporters' trusts, what do we need them for, the idea of QPR First running the club, it's ludicrous. Well, why? Why is it? What can these other people offer, then? You know?

Tracy uses the personal collective to refer to fanbases, and specifies that football clubs are not simply businesses, but are 'our clubs'. She introduces an undefined 'Other' as well here – 'people' question the purposes of supporters' trusts, and those 'people' could be either fans unconvinced of the merits of joining the organisation, or club executives unconvinced of the value of working with them or indeed wary of working with them. Similarly, when she questions what 'these other people' can offer, she could be asking whether other fans have any better ideas for collective action than via a supporters' trust, whether the current club hierarchy has any better suggestions for listening to supporters' voices, or what other potential club owners could offer that would be better than involving fans in decision making. Regardless, the 'Other' is defined in opposition to the 'us' of QPR First and the collective fanbase.

Tracy is reflective about her own femaleness as an aspect of her football supporting, and is most explicit about how she feels being female has affected other fans' attitudes towards her. She believes that taking a public role, as she has done with the trust, has directed sexism towards her, which she had never experienced previously as an 'ordinary' fan. However, when she relates her experience, her anecdotes do not indicate that other fans specifically objected to her as a woman, but that they did not agree with the idea of a supporters' trust, as shown in this extract:

> Tracy – I think also, dare I say it, I think one of the initial problems with QPR 1st as well was that in the initial stages when we were setting it up, there was myself and two other female supporters. We did meet with some resistance, shall we say, about, well, you know, there was a feeling that because we were more vocal and outspoken and because we're females and we were coming up against a little bit of resistance with that as well, we were finding – Not so much now. I think that attitudes have moved on now. But before, there were problems in that respect. We did actually come across people who were, "No, what does that silly bitch think she's talking about? Blah blah blah. We don't need QPR 1st, what do we need you for, people like you telling us what's good for the club?" Well, you know...
> CD – Had you had anything like that before your involvement with the Trust, like just at matches?
> Tracy – No, to be fair, no. Not really...

Rex Nash[4] suggests that in the independent supporters' associations he researched, female members and committee officers were reluctant to speak in meetings or in public, so it is possible that Tracy was indeed judged for transgressing norms of female behaviour. However, based on this anecdote, I suggest that other QPR fans may have objected to 'people like Tracy', but that does not necessarily mean that they objected to her femaleness. Tracy illustrates only that they did not like being told what was 'right' for the club (possibly because this would certainly affect their practices and performances of fandom). It is Tracy herself who has surmised that her being female was an element in their objection. Of course, it is possible that it was and that she has based this assumption on other separate incidents, but according to this one anecdote, there seems to be no evidence for it; at the most, her femaleness has been used as an additional reason to criticise and insult her, which is not quite the same.

5. Kimberley and Sarah: Watford

Kimberley took on an ancillary administrative role when her club's supporters' trust began, while working full-time in a senior executive fundraising position. She recalls:

> There was a big meeting being organised at the Leveret Leisure
> Centre in Watford, and I can't remember how but I ended up
> agreeing to take the minutes, and I can't quite remember how
> that happened.

Because Kimberley is so vague about the chain of events that led to her taking the minutes, it is difficult to infer the reasons behind it with any degree of accuracy. This allocation of roles shows that Kimberley (not an administrator by profession) takes on a traditionally female task; and it is also worth noting that the minute-taker's chances for contributing to the discussion are limited, because her focus is on recording the contributions of others. Though this may not have been a conscious reasoning behind Kimberley being asked to take on this role, the end result is the same – muting, if not completely silencing, the voice of a female fan. After the trust had been officially launched, the male-led committee took note of Kimberley's professional skills. She says:

> Eventually the board of the trust asked if I was willing to be
> coopted on to the board as fundraising or whatever, and I agreed.
> It was just a matter of knowing the right people, them knowing
> me, and I'd been doing bits and bobs.

Kimberley's narrative describing how she became involved with the trust is rather brief and straightforward, encompassing the initial meeting, her role there, and then how her role changed to take into account her abilities once the trust hierarchy knew her, without making any explicit connections between her femaleness and her role in the trust. Yet her close friend Sarah, with whom she sits at home games, has a rather different view. Her work has led her to become very involved with Watford's local community, and her field of expertise is in the town's history, marketing and promotional activities, and fundraising event organisation. Sarah remembers their initial contact with the supporters' trust very differently, saying:

> Myself, actually, and my friend Kim (…) we said, well, look, two of us between us have got loads of marketing experiene (…) She knows about fundraising, she knows about local community groups, she's a known face. Then you had me who is known for doing football things, straight off the back of two big football exhibitions, who sort of knows lots of people. I work for the local council. I know a lot of the community groups. So we said, well, look, between us, we have a load of local knowledge, can we help, we really want to be part of this (…). We basically got palmed off on this sub-marketing committee, on this guy, who's really nice, but he worked for eBay. It was like, great, utilise him, but he didn't have any marketing.

Sarah goes as far to make the connection between the problems she faced (and that she assumes Kimberley faced too) with the supporters' trust board and a sexist mindset. She says:

> We were thinking, we're here, we really want to be taken seriously. I actually wrote to the trust, or emailed these guys and said that I really feel some of this is because we are female and we were not being taken seriously. You got the impression that they thought we should just go off and do a cake stall. That, I was angry about.

She sarcastically suggests here that the men on the board thought the women should 'do a cake stall'; that is, fit in to a traditionally 'female', 'domestic' role, and provide a fundraising, 'supportive' element to the trust's activities. Unsurprisingly, her anger and disappointment has led to generally negative views about the trust itself. She does not refer to it in inclusive terms, as an organisation to which she belongs and is a part, but uses the pronoun 'they' to refer to the trust as a whole but more specifically the board members, distancing herself from it and from them. It is evident that she does not agree with the way the trust is being run or its priorities. As she puts it:

> From my perspective, I don't, I've not really enjoyed the supporters' trust as much as I hoped I would do. I felt at the beginning, really positive, that it was something I could do. It's kind of got down the road to other things that have been done before. They're having trouble now getting people to stay as members, because people have lost that emergency – they've missed a lot of bandwagon, they've missed their chance. Also, there's that idea that they have a lot of meetings with the club

that they're not allowed to talk about, this inner sanctum. The
club refers to an inner sanctum. I think that's really, really shaky.
I think that's more shaky for the supporters' trust to have that
inner sanctum feel. OK, I could have been on that committee.
Maybe I could have been in that inner sanctum. That wasn't the
point for me.

She explains here that she was hoping to 'enjoy' being part of the supporters'
trust and the new opportunities it offers for fan involvement rather than imitating
previous supporters groups' activities. She did not want to be involved in order to
discover confidential information about the club or to be closer to its personnel; for
her, such motivations are 'shaky' and not 'the point'. I suggest that 'the point' for
her was her wish to be part of a significant cooperative collective, which could take
effective action due to its collaborative ethos.

6. Conclusion

Although English football clubs have been traditionally owned by rich
individuals and consortiums, there has been a recent change whereby supporters
have been able to become more involved and develop closer ties with their clubs
and the local community.[5] Though the democratic nature of the supporters' trust
movement, and its stated aim of looking to the future and preserving football clubs
in their home communities for generations to come, theoretically offers new
opportunities for all fans to become involved in the life of their club, the
experience of female fans does not necessarily indicate that this is either easy or
without issues of sexism.

As I have shown, respondents involved in the supporters' trust movement
commented on the particularly 'gendered' roles assumed by people within the
movement, and how they felt they were perceived by male fellow fans, with some
feeling that putting oneself in a more visible role within the fanbase opens them up
to sexism. I have drawn parallels with the 'support' roles women seem to be
expected to take in supporters' movements (as opposed to roles that put them in the
public eye), and the 'support' roles women are expected to take in other situations,
such as within the domestic sphere and in conversation.

Notes

[1]   Susan Ward, 2010, 'What Alternative Business Models Exist in the
Organisation of Professional Football Clubs?' Viewed 26 July 2012,
http://www.ribm.mmu.ac.uk/symposium2010/extendedabstract/Ward%20Sara.pdf.
[2]   Personal correspondence with author.
[3]   Office of National Statistics, 2003, 'A Century of Labour Market Change',
viewed 10 May 2012,

http://www.statistics.gov.uk/articles/labour_market_trends/century_labour_market
_change_mar2003.pdf.
[4]   Rex Nash, 'Fan Power: The FA Premier League, Fandom and Cultural
Contestation in the 1990s' (PhD diss,. University of Liverpool, 1999).
[5]   Rogan Taylor, *Football and Its Fans: Supporters and Their Relations with the
Game* (Leicester: University Press, 1992); Nash, 'Fan Power'.

Bibliography

Brown, Adam. '"Our Club, Our Rules": Fan Communities at FC United of
Manchester.' *Soccer & Society* 9.3 (2008): 346-358.

Cleland, Jamie A. 'From Passive to Active: The Changing Relationship between
Supporters and Football Clubs'. *Soccer & Society* 11.5 (2010): 537-552.

Coddington, Anne. *One of the Lads: Women Who Follow Football.* London:
HarperCollins, 1997.

Farrell, Annemarie, Janet Fink and Sarah Fields, 'Women's Sport Spectatorship:
An Exploration of Men's Influence.' *Journal of Sport Management* 25 (2011):
190-201.

Free, Marcus and John Hughson. 'Settling Accounts with Hooligans: Gender
Blindness in Football Supporter Subculture Research.' *Men and Masculinities* 6
(2003): 136.

Jones, Katharine. 'Female Fandom: Identity, Sexism and Men's Professional
Football in England.' *Sociology of Sport Journal* 25 (2008): 516-537.

Martin, Paul. 'Football, Community and Cooperation: A Critical Analysis of
Supporter Trusts in England.' *Soccer & Society* 8.4 (2007): 636-653.

Nash, Rex. 'Fan Power: The FA Premier League, Fandom and Cultural
Contestation in the 1990s'. PhD diss. University of Liverpool, 1999.

———. 'The Sociology of English Football in the 1990s: Fandom, Business and
Future Research.' *Football Studies* 3.1 (2000): 49-63.

Taylor, Rogan. *Football and Its Fans: Supporters and Their Relations with the
Game.* Leicester: University Press, 1992.

Ward, Susan. 'What Alternative Business Models Exist in the Organisation of Professional Football Clubs?' 2010. Viewed 26 July 2012.
http://www.ribm.mmu.ac.uk/symposium2010/extendedabstract/Ward%20Sara.pdf.

Polish Football under Transition: Catch-Up Modernisation Gone Wrong

Wojciech Woźniak

Abstract
The second half of the 20th century witnessed the transformation of football from 'the people's game' – an egalitarian entertainment for the masses, with weekend games being important parts of the daily routines of working class males – to one of the crucial spheres of global show business producing enormous profits. Neoliberalisation, commercialisation and hypercommodification of the game were among key terms used to describe processes occurring in the capitalist world of football which has been carefully studied by many scholars (with particular academic input provided by British authors). The situation of sport as a whole, and of football in particular in the countries which for half a century remained trapped on the other side of the iron curtain, was entirely different; therefore the transformation of football and its culture there happened at another pace and had other implications. For various reasons this has remained outside the area of interest of scholars who in many cases simply omitted Eastern Europe in their considerations.[1] The chapter presents in a comprehensive and synthetic manner some of the peculiar phenomena of catch-up transformations in Polish football. Attempts to follow the Western model of commodification were hampered both by the inefficiency and corruption present within the Polski Związek Piłki Nożnej (Polish Football Association, hereafter: PZPN), and by some of the flows inherent in the mode of the neoliberalisation of football, promoted naively by media and elites. Attention is also paid to the issues of football hooliganism and spectatorship in general and its portrayal in mass-media as one of the important features of symbolic cultural wars.

Key Words: Catch-up modernisation, corruption, democratic transition, fandom, football, hooliganism, modernisation, Poland, spectatorship, transformation.

*****

When Poland entered the capitalist world after the decades spent under Soviet dominance, modernisation was a key goal steering the process of democratic transition after years of stagnation. This has also applied to the world of sport, where the already highly commercialised football of Western Europe was perceived as an exemplary outcome of desired reform. Media formulated one possible way of achieving success, through the implementation of market-driven reforms. Expectations were fuelled without paying attention to the national context or to specific features of the catch-up modernisation occurring in the nineties. I argue that in many respects this discourse of modernisation was in essence a false promise made by elites and believed by the general public in a time of neoliberal market euphoria. From the institutional perspective, and regardless of market failures, it seems likely that the prevalence of old structures among sport's professional associations was a serious obstacle to reforming the system of football's organisation within a social reality entirely different to that of communist times. Due to its brief size, this chapter attempts to point out the main processes occurring in Polish football throughout the transition period, rather than offering a wide and holistic discussion. Thus, it is descriptive rather than exploratory in nature, considering *some* phenomena which to some extent might be seen as representative of the situation in post-Socialist Europe.[2]

1. Football behind the Iron Curtain: False Amateurs and Real Successes

In order to discuss the transformation process, we need to consider the specificity of its starting point. In all countries of the Eastern Bloc, sport was heavily used as an invaluable tool for propaganda purposes and the 'continuation of politics by the other means'. On one hand, as Garry Whanel puts it: 'The communist countries of eastern Europe consciously adopted a policy of proving communist superiority by outstripping the Western nations in Olympic performance, a goal which they have achieved remarkably successfully.'[3] On the other hand, sport supervised and controlled by the state served as a perfect 'opiate of the masses' in the societies stripped of many other forms of entertainment or activity.

Officially, sport in the Soviet bloc was of the amateur variety.[4] As with many other features of life under communist rule, a different reality lay behind the facade. Most officially amateur football players playing in the top division were employed in state-owned enterprises on false contracts, being paid for blue collar work or military/police service work which they did not in fact carry out.[5]

Even though top footballers were not allowed to move to play in the Western European leagues (until they turned 30) or make decent money officially, in a declaratively classless socialist society they belonged to the privileged group, far better off than the working class and intelligentsia. One of the top Polish players from the eighties, the late Włodzimierz Smolarek who earned 60 caps for Poland, recalls in his biography that in the beginning of that decade footballers in Widzew Łódź were earning on average 6 times more than their blue collar working parents (who in the society praising the working class and manual labour were paid similarly to the educated professionals). What was even more important in the socialist shortage economy, was that they had permanent access to scarce goods such as flats or cars, and a tight social network of contacts with privileged people from nomenklatura circles.[6] Andrzej Iwan, another top Polish player from this era underlines another aspect of this situation. Many clubs were closely connected to the military or security services of the communist state. In his autobiography, Iwan claims:

Whether one likes it or not, Wisła Kraków was a *militsiya* (communist police) club. In Górnik Zabrze footballers were given contracts as miners, in Legia Warsaw they were able to serve to lieutnant in the army and in Wisła they were on a payroll of *Służba bezpieczeństwa* (Security Service of the Ministry of Internal Affairs)'.[7]

The system worked generally well in terms of sporting results. Polish fans are still proud to have twice as many medals from FIFA World Cups than does the 'cradle of football' (England), finishing third in 1974 and again in 1982. Many clubs were closely and formally associated with factories. Łódź, as a centre of textile industry, financed its club through its textile manufactures; clubs from the Upper Silesia were financed in a large part from coal export; and those from Gdańsk and Gdynia were closely connected to the shipbuilding industry. The demise of *ancien régime* brought plenty of challenges. Publicly subsidised clubs were no longer able to live at the expense of the military and industrial complex. Rapid deindustrialisation left many of them without sufficient means to maintain their previous positions.

2. The Nineties: Misery on the Pitch, Riot on the Stands

For Polish fans, the nineties began in a hopeful manner, with Legia Warszawa qualifying to the semi-finals of Cup Winners Cup in 1991 and Poland's under 21 team winning silver at the 1992 Olympic Games. These remained the top international success stories for Polish fans for the next two decades. The subsequent year was marked with one of the most depressing victories ever when Jan Furtok secured 1-0 against San Marino scoring by hand. After playing in the four subsequent FIFA World Cups between 1974-1986, the national team failed to qualify for any major tournament for the next 16 years, dropping out at the group stage from the each and every one afterwards. The 1996-1997 season was the second – and the last – in which the Polish team featured in the Champions League. That the last goal of a Polish player was scored in the Premier League is further evidence of the decline of Polish football – on the 19th of August 1992, Robert Warzycha of Everton contributed to a 3-0 away victory over Manchester United.

In parallel, the number of violent incidents at the stands increased. One of the first known large scale cases was a riot between Lech Poznań and Legia Warszawa in Częstochowa in 1980 where at least one fan was killed and hundreds were injured. However, no official data was made available afterwards and the story has been suppressed. Thus, researchers tend to rely on the accounts of first-hand witnesses to these events. The beginning of the nineties was marked by a significant growth in football-related violence, particularly in the rapidly de-industrialising cities, a fact which corresponds well with traditional Marxist explanations of this phenomenon. Sky-rocketing unemployment, anomy, a lack of security and stabilisation together with increased risk and the polarisation of society provided conditions for the growth of various pathologies – among them, football hooliganism. The scarce empirical studies conducted in the field correspond well with other accounts of football hooliganism in Eastern Europe.[8] The emergence of a football-related violence was probably delayed in police states of this region due to the rigorous control, but it is also likely that any incidents were not allowed to make it to the headlines due to state censorship and restricted media coverage.

3. Old Habits Die Long

This period is also perceived as a one marked with large amounts of corruption. However, the structural and normative circumstances which allowed this situation date back to communist times. Lack of democratisation and state control over the demoralized, yet powerful institutional structures managing football leagues allowed the rise of corruption. This phenomenon will remain a public secret forever, as only then Polish penal code was supplemented with special regulations defining corruption in sport as punishable by a criminal offence. Two years later an enormous scandal was ignited by the press interview with one of the former club's chairmen admitted to collaboration with public prosecutors as a witness testifying against people involved in corruption in the top flight of Polish football. Subsequently 372 persons were persecuted and as for August 2012, 242 are already convicted. Among them were: former coach of the national team, members of the PZPN board, referees, active and retired footballers, coaches.[9] 73 clubs were involved in corruption with 13 being punished with relegations by the PZPN. At the same time subsequent Polish governments were trying to force PZPN to implement reforms, e.g. preventing compromised persons from occupying top positions in the association. None of the attempts proved successful. All were hampered by the supranational bodies (FIFA and UEFA) which compelled any form of external intervention into independent body of PZPN. Contrary to the other fields of social reality, media control in case of PZPN did not work at all.

4. Neoliberal False Promise

The fear of hooliganism was one of the reasons why large private investors in the nineties were eager to finance clubs from smaller towns. New clubs appeared in Grodzisk Wielkopolski (app. 14 thousand inhabitants) Pniewy (7 thousand) Wronki (12 thousand). Some relative successes (victories in Polish cups) were challenged with lack of fans and none of the clubs are still present in Poland's top division. Licenses to play in top division and participate in European competitions were sold to the investors who have decided to buy the clubs with longer history and more potential in terms of fanbase and franchise marketing. In a highly questionable manner (similar to the UK's case of Milton Keynes replacing

Wimbledon) Lech Poznan and Polonia Warszawa replaced accordingly Amica Wronki and Groclin Grodzisk Wielkopolski.

For the Polish football league, the nineties was a decade marked by many scandals, and by the presence of some very suspicious businessmen. The media rightly pointed to a lack of clear rules, and to imprecise legislation in respect to both sport as a whole and to club ownership in particular, as disincentives to investors. Nonetheless, in 1997, Wisła Kraków – as the very first Polish club – was purchased by Bogusław Cupiał, one of Poland's richest men. It was turned into a transparent stock company. Since then, many major clubs have been taken over by leading entrepreneurs who feature on lists of 'the 100 wealthiest Poles' – for example, Widzew Łódź, Polonia Warszawa, Legia Warszawa, Śląsk Wrocław, Lech Poznań and Cracovia Kraków. The presumption that football is a business like any other and that it would be possible to repeat Premier League-style expansion in the Polish context was shared by those entering the football business.

The Director of the board of Legia Warszawa after the club was taken over by the media holding ITI (owner of popular entertainment TV channel TVN) claimed:

> Legia works exactly like the television. The goals are analogous – we produce content. In the club it is a game, in TV a show or a series. Then, we sell it to those paying tickets (…). I am sometimes accused that I treat a game like it was something similar to 'Dancing with Stars'. That's exactly how it is from the perspective of the business.[10]

In some cases this kind of approach led to relative successes on a national scale; yet no international triumphs have been achieved by Polish clubs. In many cases public resources are still used to support private enterprises. Regardless of the private ownership of the clubs, the renovation or construction of the stadia of Śląsk, Lech and Lechia Gdańsk (all used during EURO 2012), as well as those in Kraków (Cracovia and Wisła) and Warszawa (Legia), was subsidised or financed entirely by the local authorities of the corresponding cities.

As attendances declined steadily, it emerged that many Polish supporters were not willing to participate in live games, believing that stadia had become dangerous places. From time to time – when some spectacular (or spectacularly exaggerated) disaster occurred – public opinion would enter a period of what might be termed full-blown moral panic, directed against 'the savages at the stands.' Exactly like the Polish hooligans who sought inspiration in the UK's 'golden era' of football hooliganism, the Polish elite sought inspiration in the British experience about how to overcome these problems. Catch-up modernisation was in this respect pure imitation.

However, the decision makers tended to be very selective, implementing only the most rigid and punitive solutions rather than any 'soft' measures. CCTV monitoring systems were installed and police forces were provided with additional emergency powers. Very strict identification schemes were imposed which forced all supporters to purchase ID cards comprising a photograph and private data. Every person wishing to buy a ticket for a league game must possess a 'fan card' – showing affiliation with the host club – and present their ID document upon entry to the ground. This means, for instance, that supporters from Łódzkie province are unable to purchase an individual one-off match ticket for a game in Warszawa even when the Łódzkie team are playing there. Clubs are entitled and even encouraged to impose bans on misbehaving supporters, which includes not only 'hooligans' and those engaged in fighting, but also fans committing more minor offenses such as cursing at the referee or trespassing the stands. The introduction of these radical measures was not debated at all publicly in terms of civil rights, privacy or data protection, and was accompanied by misleading assurances that 'this is how it is done in Europe' – with false arguments about a complete demise of football-related violence in the 'civilised' West. A justifiable desire to counteract racist or xenophobic behaviours at the stands turned into an excuse to forbid any kind of political declarations by fans. Sometimes this over-zealousness can lead to bizarre situations – for example, supporters from Warszawa were once prevented from commemorating the memory of soldiers and civilians killed during the Warsaw Uprising of 1944.

János Bali recounts a massive critical response from the public in Hungary against attacks made in the foreign press against Hungarian supporters.[11] Meanwhile, the Polish mass media were unanimously vocal in *accepting* criticism coming from abroad. The alleged rise of Polish hooliganism was also one of few topics being reported in international academic work considering football and Poland. Polish hooligans were doubtless appreciative of this attention; their ultimate point of reference was the 'British disease' of a decade earlier, and they hoped to becomes as widely known and as widely feared. Steve Redhead recalls that fear of Polish hooligans (as shown in some critical works by Polish, German and English scholars) was usually exaggerated, often being fuelled by tabloid newspapers prior to games between Poland and England or Germany.[12]

Orientalist attitudes or a stigmatisation of Eastern Europeans as a threat was not met with criticism by the mainstream Polish media. A negative image of Polish fans – as displayed during games by both the Polish national team and smaller clubs – were perceived as proof of the fans' cultural and civilisational backwardness.[13] This view was also embraced to a large extent by the general public, who supported radical political actions being taken against a wider group of 'hoodies.' In several cases it was the involvement of organised supporters' groups that prevented the demise of their clubs. Pogoń Szczecin, GKS Katowice, ŁKS Łódź, Widzew Łódź, Hutnik Kraków, Zagłębie Sosnowiec and Polonia Warszawa; all once powerful and successful clubs, representing Poland in European competitions – and all, during the last decade, falling under the serious threat of collapse. Those collapses were prevented due to the actions of well organised fan groups. They rarely however garnered attention or praise in the mainstream media.

Ironically, the very same media which were usually so critical of supporters seemed eager to repeat British press reports praising the Polish style of match-day celebration. The way that supporters of Lech Poznań and Wisła Kraków conducted themselves during games against Manchester City and Fulham was appreciated by British fans and the British media – which seemed to begin a bizarre *legitimisation* of their 'ultras' style of support in the eyes of Polish journalists.

The process described by Steve Redhead as the 'bourgeoisification' of the game and the transformation of 'soccer into pop' was perceived as a positive one.[14] A newly established middle class was expected to fill the stands and replace the uncivilised traditional 'die-hard' fan base. The promise of 'civilised', well off and consumption-oriented supporters remains unfulfilled. Members of the middle class have become – to use the taxonomy offered by Richard Giulianotti – 'flâneurs' or 'followers'.[15] They choose freely their club allegiance, preferring to spend money on global franchises. Instead of visiting the stands of a local club, they go once or twice a season to watch Barcelona live at Camp Nou, weekly following their games on TV. The topic of blossoming organised groups following top European clubs is still under researched, but preliminary findings show a quite gloomy perspective for Polish clubs in this competition. The groups of industrial die-hard fans – to use an expression offered by Kossakowski, Antonowicz and Szlendak[16] – still constitute a significant share of attendance at the stands and remain important sources of income for them. The conflict around Legia Warszawa between fans and the owners proved that getting rid of the traditional fandom could simply devastate club's budgets while the promise of well off newcomers remains in vain.

5. Conclusion

This brief sketch of the processes occurring within Polish football support in a period of democratic transition has pointed at some particularities of the situation which have most likely significantly hampered both the modernisation of football and its radical commercialisation. The enthusiastic embrace of democratic principles in Poland at the beginning of the nineties was inherently intertwined in public discourse with an uncritical praise of neoliberal economic solutions. Social groups which in some way opposed this new order were usually stigmatised and attempts were made to strip them of their influence. Interestingly, against the wishful thinking of a powerful media and despite an indifferent public, traditional football supporters are among those who have managed to retain some significance, in contrast with trade unions or many other special interest groups. Unsurprisingly, yet unexpectedly for some, the globalisation of football works in favour of a *global* market, not local franchises. While Poland's new market-oriented football clubs began trying to attracted new fans, those fans had already declared their allegiances to global brands elsewhere. Regardless of the failure of neoliberalism's promise, it must be emphasised that the obsolete functioning style of Polish football was for many years deeply rooted in a communist heritage which hampered significant reforms. This situation was worsened by institutional umbrellas provided by organisations like FIFA and UEFA – which defend the sovereignty of national football associations no matter how detrimental the pathological conditions are that result from their actions.

Notes

[1] See for example: Anastassia Tsoukala, *Football Hooliganism in Europe. Security and Civil Liberties in the Balance* (Houndmills, New York: Palgrave Macmillan, 2009), 11.

[2] I will not go into details of the situation after the year 2007. This is the year that Poland and the Ukraine were appointed as hosts of the 2012 UEFA European Football Championships. This created a new momentum in Poland, both in politics, as well as in sport and public discourse surrounding football issues. It certainly deserves separate analysis which will be provided elsewhere.

[3] Garry Whanel, *Culture, Politics and Sport: Blowing the Whistle Revisited* (Oxon, New York: Routledge, 2008), 45. Regardless of official propaganda, for many football supporters games within the family of socialist countries were the most important hallmarks of competition. Certainly the most crucial ones concerned rivalry with the Eastern 'big brother'. For example in Poland's case, there were very few victories against the Soviet Union. These were: the first post-war victory in football in 1957 (2-1 in a qualifier for World Cup 1958), the only triumph in ice-hockey during the World Championships in 1976, and the Olympic volleyball final in the same year (won 3-2). These became legendary moments known and repeatedly remembered as *politically defined* sport victories.

[4] In case of football it had interesting implications, as the national teams from the Eastern bloc contrary to those from the Western bloc were able to compete in Olympic Games. Consequently 23 out of 27 medals between 1948 and 1980 were won by Eastern Europe with gold in 1972 and silver and 1976 by Poland. It is quite symbolic that during Olympic Games in 1980 – 4 countries which competed in the semi-finals just a little more than a decade later vanished from the map of Europe (Czechoslovakia, Soviet Union, East Germany and Yugoslavia).

[5] Author of this chapter recalls firsthand relations from his grandfather who while working as an accountant in one of the largest cotton factories in the city of Łódź was officially a colleague of Jan Tomaszewski, Polish legendary goalkeeper. The 'man who stopped England' was formally employed in the same factory. The only time when the player used to appear there was while getting his wage and during festive meetings with a crew after successful come backs from the tournaments (to present medals and tell the stories).

[6] Jacek Perzyński, *Smolar. Piłkarz z charakterem* (English title: *Smolar. Footballer with Charisma*) (Warszawa: Instytut Wydawniczy ERICA, 2012), 116-117.

[7] Andrzej Iwan and Krzysztof Stanowski, *Spalony. Autobiografia* (English title: *Offsided. Autobiography*. Warszawa: Buchmann, 2012), 62-63. The repercussions of this situation are still present in the inherited collective memory of supporters. Many still refer to the fact that coaches of Legia Warszawa were able and eager to use their military status to call up for military service any talented player from all over the country. Others point at the dark heritage of communist secret services who were closely connected to another clubs or to the privileges of teams from Upper Silesia whose bosses during the seventies were top 'players' in the Central Committee of the communist party, which significantly favoured their favourite clubs.

[8] See: Jerzy Dudała, *Fani-chuligani. Rzecz o polskich kibolach* (English title: *Fans-Hooligans: About Polish Hools*) (Warszawa: Wydawnictwo Akademickie Żak, 2004), 36-40, 52; Przemysław Piotrowski, 'Soccer Hooliganism in Poland: Its Extent, Dynamism and Psycho-Social Conditions,' in *(Re)Constructing Cultures of Violence and Peace*, ed. Richard Jackson (Amsterdam and New York: Rodopi), 79-81. Both authors are among very few sociologists delivering any kind of sociological inquiry into the world of sport, yet their research enterprise was strictly limited to the field of sports hooliganism. See also: Ramón Spaaij, *Understanding Football Hooliganism* (Amsterdam: Amsterdam University Press, 2006), 324; Vic Duke and Pavel Slepička, 'Bohemian Rhapsody: Football Supporters in the Czech Republic,' in *Fighting Fans: Football Hooliganism as a World Phenomenon*, ed. Eric Dunning, Patrick Murphy, Ivan Waddington and Antonios E. Astrinakis (Dublin: University College Dublin Press, 1984), 49-61.

[9] Most prominent ones included: Janusz Wójcik, former manager of the national team and trophy winning coach of Legia Warszawa, Dariusz Wdowczyk, former Celtic Glasgow player and coach of Polonia Warszawa when the club won Polish Championships in 2000, Łukasz Piszczek right-back from Borussia Dortmund currently playing for a national team, and Wit Żelazko longstanding head of department of refereeing in PZPN and leading TV pundit in this field. For the most up to date, comprehensive and detailed data on corruption in Polish football see the blog of radio journalist Dominik Panek meaningfully titled 'football mafia': Dominik Panek, *Piłkarska mafia* (blog), last modified August 12, 2012, accessed August 13, 2012, http://pilkarskamafia.blogspot.com/.

[10] Radosław Kossakowski, Dominik Antonowicz and Tomasz Szlendak, 'Ostatni bastion antykonsumeryzmu? Kibice industrialni w dobie komercjalizacji sportu' (English title: The Last Bastion of Anti-Consumerism: Industrial Die-Hard-Fans and the Commercialization of Sport), *Studia Socjologiczne* 3 (2010): 113.

[11] See: János Bali, 'Ferencváros, Hungary and the European Champions League: The Symbolic Construction of Marginality and Exclusion,' in *Fear and Loathing*

in World Football, ed. Gary Armstrong and Richard Giulianotti (Oxford, New York: Berg, 2001), 254-262.

[12] See: Steve Redhead, *Post-Fandom and the Millenial Blues* (London, New York: Routledge, 2003), 14; Martina Schreiber and Otto Adang, 'The Poles are Coming! Fan Behaviour and Police Tactics around the World Cup Match Germany vs. Poland (Dortmund, 14 June 2006),' *Sport in Society* 13.4 (2010): 470-488; Joseph Maguire, Zbigniew Mazur, Irmina Wawrzyczek, Richard Elliott, 'New Europe, Old Games? Making Sense of Anglo-Polish Media Coverage of England versus Poland Football Matches,' *Sport in Society* 12.2 (2009): 141-155.

[13] See for example an article published in one of the English tabloids, subsequently quoted by all major media in Poland: Jenna Sloan, 'Do the Poznan', *The Sun*, last modified February 21, 2011, accessed August 13, 2012, http://www.thesun.co.uk/sol/homepage/features/3389828/Man-City-fans-are-doing -the-Poznan.html.

[14] Redhead, *Post-Fandom and the Millenial Blues*, i.

[15] Richard Giulianotti, 'Supporters, Followers, Fans and Flaneurs: A Taxonomy of Spectator Identities in Football', *Journal of Sport and Social Issues* 26.1 (2002): 25-46.

[16] Radosław Kossakowski, Dominik Antonowicz and Tomasz Szlendak, 'Ostatni bastion antykonsumeryzmu? Kibice industrialni w dobie komercjalizacji sportu'.

Bibliography

Bali, János. 'Ferencváros, Hungary and the European Champions League: The Symbolic Construction of Marginality and Exclusion,' In *Fear and Loathing in World Football*, edited by Gary Armstrong and Richard Giulianotti, 251-264. Oxford, New York: Berg, 2001.

Dudała, Jerzy. *Fani-chuligani. Rzecz o polskich kibolach.* Warszawa: Wydawnictwo Akademickie Żak, 2004.

Duke, Vic, and Pavel Slepička. 'Bohemian Rhapsody: Football Supporters in the Czech Republic.' In *Fighting Fans: Football Hooliganism as a World Phenomenon*, edited by Eric Dunning, Patrick Murphy, Ivan Waddington and Aantonios E. Astrinakis, 49-61. Dublin: University College Dublin Press, 1984.

Giulianotti, Richard. 'Supporters, Followers, Fans and Flaneurs: A Taxonomy of Spectator Identities in Football.' *Journal of Sport and Social Issues* 26.1 (2002): 25-46.

Iwan, Andrzej and Krzysztof Stanowski. *Spalony. Autobiografia.* Warszawa: Buchmann, 2012.

Kossakowski, Radosław, Dominik Antonowicz and Tomasz Szlendak Tomasz. 'Ostatni bastion antykonsumeryzmu? Kibice industrialni w dobie komercjalizacji sportu.' *Studia Socjologiczne* 3 (2010): 113-139.

Maguire, Joseph, Zbigniew Mazur, Irmina Wawrzyczek and Richard Elliott. 'New Europe, Old Games? Making Sense of Anglo-Polish Media Coverage of England versus Poland Football Matches.' *Sport in Society* 12.2 (2009): 141-155.

Panek, Dominik, *Piłkarska mafia* (blog). http://pilkarskamafia.blogspot.com/.

Perzyński, Jacek. *Smolar. Piłkarz z charakterem.* Warszawa: Instytut Wydawniczy ERICA, 2012.

Piotrowski, Przemysław. 'Soccer Hooliganism in Poland: Its Extent, Dynamism and Psycho-Social Conditions.' In *(Re)Constructing Cultures of Violence and Peace*, edited by R. Jackson, 79-90. Amsterdam and New York: Rodopi, 2004.

Redhead, Steve. *Post-Fandom and the Millenial Blues.* London, New York: Routledge, 2003.

Schreiber, Martina, and Otto Adang. 'The Poles are Coming! Fan Behaviour and Police Tactics around the World Cup Match Germany vs. Poland (Dortmund, 14 June 2006).' *Sport in Society* 13.4 (2010): 470-488.

Sloan, Jenna. 'Do the Poznan.' *The Sun*, last modified February 21, 2011. Accessed August 13, 2012. http://www.thesun.co.uk/sol/homepage/features/3389828/Man-City-fans-are-doing -the-Poznan.html

Spaaij, Ramón. *Understanding Football Hooliganism.* Amsterdam: Amsterdam University Press, 2006

Tsoukala, Anastassia. *Football Hooliganism in Europe: Security and Civil Liberties in the Balance.* Houndmills, New York: Palgrave Macmillan, 2009.

Whanel, Garry. *Cuture, Politics and Sport: Blowing the Whistle Revisited.* Abingdon, New York: Routledge, 2008.

Polish Supporters the Day before Euro 2012: Historical and Sociological Draft

Jacek Burski

Abstract
In this chapter, I offer a socio-historical analysis of the main trends of change occurring in the social world of football supporters in Poland over the last two decades, which have seen emerging modern supporting behaviours manifest themselves in accordance with specific local contexts. This period is divided here into three main phases, each of which is strongly connected to historical episodes which are in some way turning points in the history of Polish football spectatorship. Furthermore, every period is defined by specific features which afterwards have become an element of public stereotype concerning football supporters in general.

Key Words: Football fandom, football hooliganism, Polish supporters, Ultras movements.

*****

1. Introduction

As this article was being written, the biggest sporting event ever to take place in Poland finally came to an end. The final tournament was one of the best in the history of European Championships, and the organisational side was not as bad as some critics anticipated. For Poles in general, it was a time of excitement. Yet, we can observe, in the middle of overflowing joy, shadows of doubt, negation and mutiny against Euro 2012. The biggest social source of these voices were communities of traditional football supporters organised around Polish football clubs. Strong in both the number of members[1] and in their often radical beliefs, football communities were the main critics of Euro 2012 in Poland.

What are the reasons for this attitude and, furthermore, what social causes led to a situation in which Polish supporters have become one of main *folk devils* in public debate about sport and football itself? Is it just serious involvement in violent behaviour inside and outside the stadiums? Or growing levels of engagement by fans with political debates and the entering into of alliances with right wing oriented parties? On the other hand we can observe – in terms of professionalisation and institutionalisation – structures of football supporters' communities becoming more operational and effective. At many levels these processes have made Polish supporters more responsible and stable social actors.

In the chapter, I concentrate on a socio-historical analysis of the main trends of change in the social world of football supporters in Poland over the last two decades as a time of emergence; of locally contextualised but still modern supporting. This period will be divided into three main phases, each being strongly connected with historical episodes which are in some way turning points in the history of Polish football spectatorship.

In the second part of the article I would like to present general thoughts about wider social issues (tendencies and consequences) identified as the main characteristics of the whole analysed period. In this part I underline my theoretical intuitions and briefly justify them.

2. Demons of Hooliganism

The first period described starts in 1989 and is strongly connected with macrostructural change occurring in Poland. Transformation from a socialist and autocratic state to a neoliberal and democratic one was a fundamental factor of change in Polish society, including in the world of football. Clubs had to reorient their financial policies and were required to find new economic sources if they wanted to survive. In the next few years after political change the majority of them got into financial troubles, which some of them have not overcome to this day. Struggling with economic hardship, clubs' management hierarchies weren't particularly interested in creating new spectatorship policies, leaving this on the margins of their main activities. Partly in consequence of this situation, football supporters became somewhat more autonomic both politically and culturally. It was an issue which – in the early 90s – became one of the main problems for Polish football officials: how to manage and – as sometimes prevailed – how to secure active and strong football supporter communities without getting embroiled in conflict.

Football audiences after 1989 became more and more prone to symbolic and physical aggression, rivalry between groups of fans becoming the main framework for their social relations. Before post-communist transformation, violence had occurred relatively rarely in comparison. However, the socialist state strictly censored information about football violence so that even when incidents took place, it was most likely that newspapers and public television (the only television service available in Poland at that time) would not inform citizens about it.

After 1989 we can observe the first wave of change at football stadiums. Traditional groups of supporters focused on the *game* became less influential and hooligans started to play the main role at the terraces. Similarly to the English case, an important factor in the emergence of this new style of spectatorship came from media. Slowly and insistently football stadiums became places directly connected with violence in public discourse.

One of the most common supporters' misbehaviours was pitch invasions (sometimes on a large scale). Often these actions lead to physical clashes between opposing fans or fans and police. Physical violence at this time was common and was not limited to hermetic hooligan groups (which is a special characteristic of the Polish situation). The 90s were and are seen by many die-hard supporters as a golden age in the dominant narrative discourse about the history of the movement. Relatively weak control by police and officials, lenient repressions, and a high probability of fights were the main factors that encouraged people to get into 'action.' Nevertheless we can assume that other social factors played their role in spreading the new style on the terraces. I would like to underline macrostructural elements like constant economic crises connected with political, social and economic transformations leading to high levels of unemployment and poverty. During that time, no serious research was undertaken allowing an examination of hypotheses about the connection between general conditions of socio-historical change and their impact on violent behaviour in Polish football in that time.

The symbolic end of the first analysed period is connected with changes in clubs' management in Poland. In the ten years following 1989 the Polish league started to attract bigger money (for instance a sponsorship contract with television Canal Plus was signed in 1996, the value of which increased in subsequent years). Confirmation of growing prosperity in Polish football came with the takeover of Wisła Kraków by Bogusław Cupiał, the owner of one of the biggest companies in Poland. It coincided also with change at the terraces, where the 'ultras' movement emerged to become a leading force among supporters' movements.

3. Ultras Era

After the stormy nineties, when hooligan activity was common in Polish football, the time of the ultras had arrived. At first we ought to ask what is the ultras movement? What is the main activity of ultras and what are the main characteristics of these groups?

The origins of football 'ultras' goes back to the 1960s and the first ultras groups which started to act in Italy. Originally the word referred to political groups fighting to maintain French domination in Algeria. A second meaning comes from radical and conservative groups operating in the time of the Bourbon restoration.[2]

The history of the ultras movement started in Italy when Sampdoria Genoa fans used that word for the first time. The core of ultras is incredible scrupulosity in preparing a complex choreography combining singing, flags, banners, pyrotechnics, thousands of sets of colourful cartons covering whole sectors of stadiums, etc. One Italian author quoted ultras talking about the distinction between ultras and non-ultra fans:

> As an ultra-fan I identify myself with particular way of life. We are different from ordinary supporters because of our enthusiasm and excitement. This means, obviously, rejoicing and suffering much more acutely than everybody else. So, being ultra means exaggerating feelings, from a lot of points of view.[3]

Ultras spend a lot of money and go to great lengths to express these exaggerated feelings.

The main goal of ultras is to add to football a spectacle, and elements of carnival. The movement is formed by small and well organised groups. Their members are fanatically devoted to their club and (sometimes even more importantly) to the fans' community. This kind of spectatorship is strongly related with competition and rivalry taking place between opposite groups. In the image of sport rivalry ultras are trying to establish some kind of hierarchy which contains regular rankings of ultras choreographies.

In Poland the best organised groups function within the supporters' communities of Legia Warszawa, Lech Poznań, ŁKS Łódź, and Widzew Łódź. Fast development of this movement was possible thanks to a flow of new members into the whole spectatorship movement after 2000. The Ultras trend is strongly connected with the 'digitalisation' of Polish society and the introduction of the internet as one of most important channels of communication. The latter is one of the most characteristic factors in a move from traditional fan communities limited to precisely defined time and space locations (for instance, a football match) into virtual reality environments offering new possibilities. Without the Internet, the next steps in Polish football support toward institutionalisation and formalisation would have been impossible.

In contrast to the nineties, when violence was common and occurred directly *inside* the stadiums, the next decade saw a rise in popularity of well-organised, pre-planned clashes conducted strictly within the rules (i.e. usage of knives or baseball bats is prohibited) outside of the venues.

4. Era of the Associations

Two moments in the history of Polish spectatorship could exemplify its symbolic transition towards a new level of development of fan culture. 2004 is a date chosen based on my own research – interviews which I conducted with supporters of ŁKS Łódź – and is connected with the local history of these concrete supporters' communities. 2007 is a year in which emerged conflict between owners and supporters of Legia Warszawa, one of the biggest football clubs in Poland, which dominated discourse of supporters. These dates heralded a new mode of supporters' community organisation: formal associations.

The first case mentioned above is connected with hooligans' fights which occurred in May in 2004 in Chorzów during the match between home team Ruch and ŁKS Łódź. The game was abandoned due to the scale of troubles on the terrace and on the pitch and dozens of fans were arrested by the police. In interviews many of them pointed to this moment as turning points in their support 'careers'. For several it was the moment when they decided to stop their hooligan activity. For this particular community of fans 2004 was a year when formal association becomes an important part of their social world. It was found that thanks to benefits coming from formalisation it was easier to organise help for people arrested after fights (including food, money and in some cases lawyers). Furthermore, when a specific test was passed, an association took responsibility for formal representation of the whole supporters' community in public debates. In addition members of associations organised trips for away matches which, according to new regulations set by the Polish officials, were far harder than they had been in nineties.

The growth of supporters' movements in terms of structure and organisation was a good basis from which to formalise their functioning at the level of local communities first, and secondly, at the central level. In 2007, Polish supporters created a formalised national association: the Polish Association of Supporters Associations. This institution is currently the most important formal structure in the social world of Polish fandom and has real influence on local actions and strategies taken by local communities.

2007 is also the year of another important incident: conflict between the supporters and club owners of Legia Warszawa. ITI (the telecommunication company who bought Legia in 2004) was trying to pull away from the stands hardcore fans and take tougher control of the audience after hooligans' fights which took place during the Intertoto Cup in a match with Vetra Vilnius. It has to be added that the conflict emerged during regeneration of Legia Stadium. Yet the end of the reconstruction and the need to fill the modernised stadium with people made an agreement between the two sides possible. Both had an interest in ending the conflict (supporters wanted to get back on the terraces and once again control the fanatic part of the audience, while the club wanted to increase its financial income). An important fact here is that during the whole conflict (which included boycotts, marches, anti-ITI chants and banners on display at matches etc.) the main supporters' representation was the Legia Warszawa Supporters' Association.

We can say that associations have three major functions:

Organisational – they are responsible for community organisation (for example: preparing journeys on away matches);

Representational – on the local level they negotiate with local authorities, media, and the club.

Integrative – association is a good way to make communities less vulnerable during various difficult situations such as club relegation or financial breakdown.

In the last two years this new force in the social world of Polish supporters has had to face the problem of stereotypical depictions of football fandom as violent and antisocial, as invoked by various social actors during public debates. Another strong influence on the context at this time was the then forthcoming European Championship. Polish media highlighted news items about violence at the terraces as a serious threat for the biggest event in Polish history. After massive pitch invasions at the end of the Polish Cup final in 2010, new control measures were taken by the local authorities and the police. Closing stadia and creating administrative difficulties in the organisation of football matches were the main tools used to fight against hooligans in Poland. Paradoxically, official statistics presented by police head office showed that, just before new policy emerged, the number of fights, arrested hooligans, and the general amount of trouble caused by fans had steadily decreased over the past few years. After 2010 we can observe how this trend entirely turns for worse.[4]

Euro 2012 is another turning point in the history of Polish spectatorship but, significantly, not for the supporters' community. Public opinion and institutional social actors began to recognise that football is not limited only to fanatic part of audience but can be an option for 'socially legitimised' entertainment. Whether this perception will last is a different matter.

5. Social Mechanisms and Processes

Firstly, I would like to emphasise that problems around security and surveillance which have become some of the most important issues in discussions about football audiences elsewhere, have not been considered so important in Poland, where this complex problem is very often simplified to general thoughts.[5]

More effective and deeper control of stadiums is one of the biggest priorities for match organisers, police, security staff and the constructors of new venues. Stadiums become modern panopticons with overwhelming monitoring and potency to control. But a far more important question is: where is the border between using these serious tools and systems in good faith and manipulating and actually limiting human rights? For example, open ticket sale in advance of the game is available only to the customers living in the voivodship (province) where the match is hosted. The only option for a supporter from the other area is to take part in one of the organised away game trips which are frequently cancelled due to real or alleged security threats. Every fan who wants to get to the stadium is forced to buy an identity card and provide the club with his photo, thus also officially declaring themselves a fan of a given team. Without meeting this condition, fans are not allowed to enter the stadium. Furthermore, disturbing news is coming from a growing number of cities in Poland where, although building new stadiums, away supporters are not allowed to get in for the match. The scale of these incidents is so high that we can talk about an informal strategy introduced by the authorities and police in the name of safety – i.e. for the 'normal' audience (which of course is not described, so anybody can be included or excluded from this aggregation).

Secondly, supporters' communities are more and more active outside the stadiums and the basic immediate context of a football match. Thanks to the internet and other modern facilities, being a fan is not just an event occurring on a Saturday afternoon. It has become a new kind of lifestyle. Helpful theoretical conceptions describing this process can be found in Strauss's[6] and Shibutani's[7] concept of social worlds which are framed on primary activity, key technologies, and arenas where significant meaning and mythologies are produced. Symbolically, this move beyond the primary frame of the football supporters' experience is adding a new level to the rivalry which dominated social relations in the past. A strong need to be better than the others (in terms of ultras, hooligans or in the organisational field) is one of main motive forces of institutionalisation and professionalisation.

Watching a football match is not a primary supporter activity anymore. Rivalry with opposite supporters' groups is drawing major attention from the most fanatic part of the audience. In contrary to ordinary viewers, the most active fans are concentrated on their own 'game'. This can be related to a few tendencies: the growing importance of conflict as a main frame of social relations between opposing groups, the process of professionalisation – over the years we can see how being an active supporter has started to require more resources (money, time, skills) – and identity creation. In many cases, being a football fan has become a major activity in the establishment of one's sense of 'identity.'

We can look at these three factors as intertwined tendencies which in the end add up to one historically contextualised mechanism for the deepening and structuring of new types of supporters' experience. In this sense, the cultures of ultras, hooligans and associations (in fact, borders between these types of membership in the community are blurring and changing) are different dimensions of one deep and totalising experience which without doubts should be further examined and explored.

In addition I would like to underline two another issues. The first refers to the commercialisation of football and the way in which this process is occurring in Poland. Polish football is in some ways still archaic and poorly organised. But some clubs (Lech Poznań, Legia Warszawa, Wisła Kraków) are aspiring to become recognised and successful on the European level. Reaching these goals brings the clubs' management into conflict with strong and well organised supporters' communities which are not always open to change. This structural tension is one of the most important problems which is faced at present by football clubs in Poland.

Lastly: the institutionalisation of the supporters' milieu and a panicked reaction in terms of public opinion towards violent incidents (exacerbated by their portrayal in the mass media) provides a growing level of engagement by political game players on both local and central levels. In the last two years alone we can observe how easily supporters become a subject and object of politicking. This is another issue which should be taken up for investigation by social scientists.

Notes

[1] The number of members of football supporters associations is hard to assess. The biggest organization Wiara Lecha associates about 3000 people.

[2] Polish Language Dictionary, 1300.

[3] Alessandro Dal Lago and Rocco De Biasi, 'Italian Football Fans,' in *Football, Violence and Social Identity*, ed. Richard Giulianotti (Routledge, London, 1994), 80.

[4] For more information about statistics running by Polish Police see: http://kpk.policja.gov.pl/portal/kpk/13/11/Dane_statystyczne.html.

[5] See: Przemysław Piotrowski, *Szalikowcy. O zachowaniach dewiacyjnych kibiców sportowych* (Toruń: Wydawnictwo Adam Marszałek, 2000); Tomasz Sahaj, 'Problem kibiców i pseudokibiców we współczesnym sporcie', in *Roczniki Naukowe AWF* 49 (2001); Tomasz Sahaj, *Fani futbolowi. Historyczno-społeczne zjawisko kibicowania* (Poznań: Akademia Wychowania Fizycznego im. Eugeniusza Piaseckiego, 2007).

[6] Tamotsu Shibutani, 'Reference Groups as Perspectives', in *American Journal of Sociology* 60.6 (1955).

[7] Anselm Strauss, 'A Social World Perspective', in *Studies in Symbolic Interaction* 1 (1978).

Bibliography

Antonowicz, Dominik and Łukasz Wrzesiński. 'Kibice jako wspólnota niewidzialnej religii'. *Studia socjologiczne* 1.192 (2009).

Armstrong Garry and Dick Hobbs. 'Tackled from Behind'. *Football, Violence and Social Identity*, edited by Richard Giulianotti, Norman Bonney, and Mike Hepworth. Routledge, London, 1994.

Armstrong, Gary and Richard Giulianotti. 'From another Angle: Police Surveillance and Football Supporters'. *Surveillance, Closed Circuit Television and Social Control*, edited by Clive Norris, Jade Moran, and Gary Armstrong, 113-135. Aldershot, Brookefield: Ashgate, 1998.

Bausinger, Herman. 'Małe święta na co dzień'. *Antropologia widowisk*, edited by Krystyna Damm. Wydawnictwo Uniwersytetu Warszawskiego, Warszawa, 2005.

Cohen, Stanley. *Folk Devils and Moral Panics: The Creation of the Mods and Rockers*. 3rd Edition. London, New York: Routledge, 2002.

Dal Lago, Alessandro and Rocco De Biasi. 'Italian Football Fans'. *Football, Violence and Social Identity*, edited by Richard Giulianotti. London: Routledge, 1994.

Dudała, Jerzy. *Fani-chuligani. Rzecz o polskich kibolach. Studium Socjologiczne.* Warszawa: Wyd. Akademickie Żak, 2002.

Dunning Eric, Patrick Murphy and Ivan Waddington. 'Anthropological versus Sociological Approaches to the Study of Soccer Hooliganism: Some Critical Notes'. *The Sociological Review* 3 (1991).

Dunning, Eric. *The Roots of Football Hooliganism*. London: Routledge, 1988.

Giulianotti, Richard, Norman Bonney and Mike Hepworth, eds., *Football, Violence and Social Identity*. London: Routledge, 1994.

Giulianotti Richard. *Football: A Sociology of the Global Game*. Oxford: Polity Press, 1999.

Hobbs, Dick and David Robins. 'The Boy Done Good: Football Violence, Changes and Continuities'. *Sociological Review* 39.3 (1991): 551-579.

Hughson, John. 'Among the Thugs: The New Ethnographies of Football Supporting Subcultures'. *International Review for the Sociology of Sport* 33.1 (1998): 43-57.

Marsh, Peter, Elizabeth Rosser and Rom Harre. *The Rules of Disorder*. London: Routledge, 1978.

Murphy, Patrick, John Williams and Eric Dunning. *Football on Trial: Spectator Violence and Development in the Football World*. London, 1990

Piotrowski, Przemysław. *Szalikowcy. O zachowaniach dewiacyjnych kibiców sportowych.* Toruń: Wydawnictwo Adam Marszałek, 2000.

Shibutani, Tamotsu. 'Reference Groups as Perspectives'. *American Journal of Sociology* 60.6 (1998).

Sahaj, Tomasz. 'Problem kibiców i pseudokibiców we współczesnym sporcie'. *Roczniki Naukowe AWF* 49 (2001).

————. *Fani futbolowi. Historyczno-społeczne zjawisko kibicowania.* Poznań: Akademia Wychowania Fizycznego im. Eugeniusza Piaseckiego w Poznaniu, 2007.

Strauss, Anselm. 'A Social World Perspective'. *Studies in Symbolic Interaction* 1 (1978).

Zieliński, Roman. *Liga chuliganów.* Wrocław: Chroma, 1996.

A Study of the Relationship between the Painter's Intention and the Spectator's Interpretation: Employing Methods of Social Inquiry within the Image-Field of Football Culture

Jackie West

Abstract
The primary aim in my doctoral research programme was to explore the gap between intention and interpretation in painting. This was achieved in two ways. Firstly, by building a self-reflexive account of my intentions as a painter, analysed through repeated observations of home games at Fratton Park, Portsmouth Football Club, which were later combined into paintings. Secondly, I gathered and analysed interpretations of these paintings by focus groups. I structured these focus groups around Richard Wollheim's notion of the 'adequately informed' spectator of painting. The gap between intention and interpretation is explored through the paintings that are my response to a particular cultural scene, and are then interpreted by those who are/are not familiar with it. The thesis demonstrates the development of a methodology for art practice that allows representational painting to be used as a tool for enquiry and as an embodiment of cultural knowledge. Visual research is expected to be part of an artist's process and as a tutor I ask students to consider and explore methods and processes for their own practice and as part of their process, how their artefacts might be received and how in turn, this might affect their practice. My research project originates in my practice as a representational painter and teacher of visual research.

Key Words: Painting, representational painting, football, spectatorship.

*****

1. The Project

My practice-led research project investigates the following question: What is the relationship between the intentions of a representational painter and the interpretations of differently informed spectators, using the image field[1] of football culture as a focus for the making of paintings?

Representational painting, in this context, means a combination of representing what some physical objects look like and what they signify to me, as a result of primary source observation. I wanted to investigate a process for making paintings concerned with aspects of social documentation, influenced by my involvement as a participant within a specific cultural activity, football culture, in order to improve my practice and investigate whether painting can be a tool for research.

Initially I wanted to find out more about the impact visual signs and the activities of participants from that culture had on adolescent males. The paintings were only partly based on observation and my intentions were to question and provoke thought through sign and signification. In *Pompey Boys* for example, what is the significance of the collar of the jacket being done up or undone? In *Boots* does the spectator consider the wearer of the boots?

My field of enquiry is primarily within painting, but the research problems I addressed and the methods of investigation I developed, included references to aesthetics and sociology.

2. The Theory to be Tested

In representational painting, Wollheim suggests that there is an internal spectator, a *protagonist*, who, Wollheim proposes, facilitates access to the content of the painting for an external, adequately informed spectator. Such an external spectator is able to imagine the life of the protagonist by making associations from their own experience and/or imagination. This process Wollheim calls *centrally imagining* which has two aspects, *plenitude* and *cogency*.

Plenitude is when the external spectator, perceiving that the protagonist has perceptions/feelings, interprets these perceptions/feelings.

Cogency refers to the external spectator who, in accepting *plenitude* in the *protagonist*, can imagine relating to those feelings or thoughts, even if they themselves have not had that experience.

My intention was to explore whether the participants would identify such a protagonist in the representational paintings I made and if so, does Wollheim's protagonist allow access to the content of the painting? Furthermore, does this reveal more about a chosen image field to the spectator who has no particular experience of that field?

Wollheim's theories of spectatorship allowed me to focus on the one aspect of representational painting that had until then, been assumed or supposed, namely what is communicated by an artwork and what conditions are necessary to exist to engage the 'adequately informed observer' and also what does the term 'adequately' mean in this context?

This development focussed the project within the field of painting through reflexive accounts of painting practice and reflexive critique by differently informed audiences enabling a contribution to be made to the practice of painting and how people 'read' paintings.

Wollheim did not justify his concept of the term 'adequately informed', and had simultaneously opened up the possibility for research and the gathering of evidence, and disclosed a gap in knowledge which he did not wish to explore.

I needed to consider how to organise the participants that I would invite to take part in the research, into focus groups.

It is important to state that I was not making paintings to illustrate Wollheim's theory, but testing the validity of the theory and its bearing on the 'adequately informed' spectator through the physical and intellectual aspects of painting practice.

Wollheim also addresses the artist as agent and spectator:

> *Experience is designed to carry meaning or to offer*
> *understanding – then his reliance upon the experience that he*
> *has as he paints, his dependence upon himself as spectator is*
> *heavier.*[2]

The painter must then experience the same visual field as the spectator in order for the painting to embody the knowledge of the spectator's experience. Can the painting that embodies this knowledge give a spectator ignorant of the same visual experience an awareness of the experience? By asking the spectator 'what do you see?' invites a reflexive engagement with painting. If this invitation is extended to football fans in addition to painters, an investigation can follow exploring what it is about painting that enables spectators who are 'differently informed' to contribute to the discourse about perception within painting and philosophical aesthetics.

As a philosopher interested in psychoanalysis and painting, Wollheim's interest in the perception and meaning in representational painting, came from his knowledge and field of inquiry as a philosopher. Philosophical aesthetics is not concerned with the practice of painting, but with the discourse around the philosophy of meaning. I am interested in exploring Wollheim's propositions from a painter's perspective, in other words from the standpoint of what a painting can do and what the process of painting produces, which relates the intention of the painter to the interpretation of the spectator.

It is crucial to undertake a practice survey and a literature survey and this continues throughout the PhD process.

The practice survey included:

- Painters who concern themselves with imagery from popular/football culture exploring the reception of their representational paintings.
- Representational painters who participate within a field of enquiry and make paintings concerned with that field.
- Contemporary painters who concern themselves with making paintings from data gathered in quantitative and qualitative methods of social inquiry.
- Painters who have completed PhD research projects.

The literature survey includes discourse between authorities in the fields of art history and philosophical aesthetics concerning some of Wollheim's suppositions, relevant to my enquiry.

The art historian Timothy James Clark, has asked: '*What is in the image? What's intended by it? What's the picture of? Who's the picture for? Where does content end and context begin?*'[3]

In his influential work, '*Image of the People*' (1973), Clark promotes the idea that paintings 'produce' or anticipate their audiences rather than passively reflecting them.[4] Clark's ideas cannot therefore be mapped directly onto the way the term 'target audience' is used within the field of art design and media, indicating a general need for the artist/designer to address the spectator as part of the creative process in the making of an artwork.

Questions that arose at this point include:

- What is the relationship between target audience and informed spectator?
- Is a target audience an informed spectator?
- Are the intentions of a representational painter to inform a target audience about something they already know, and
- Can a representational painting be used to inform a less well-informed spectator?

As a painter, my intention and interest is concerned with communication through painting – this obviously involves addressing differently informed spectators.

3. Methodology

As this study is interdisciplinary in nature and because of the relationship of the two aspects of 'intention' and 'interpretation', the methodology employs a multi-method approach:

Intention
- Empirical research methods; self-observation and observations of the image field (football culture)
- The Act of Painting

Interpretation
- Qualitative research methods; focus groups

Having gained support from Portsmouth Football Club, I attended home football matches for more than two seasons, enabling me to observe the image field as a passive participant.[5] These observations led to the second aspect; making paintings.

The process is concerned with my intentions as a representational painter; quotes and images from the journals were used to reveal the process, reflections and practice as the paintings were made.

As I became more informed about qualitative research methodologies, my field notes improved and I began to document my painting process. My methodology became more focused, as I became a more informed researcher and participant of the culture I was involved in.

Sketches were made to explore how drawing can inform the paintings, my observations and the experience (gained by time and practice) descriptive notes in my journal became more significant as references to colour, atmosphere and tension were documented. Secondly, the weather conditions, which were generally cold and windy, sketching becomes increasingly difficult in such conditions and the use of a digital video recorder became more important. The conclusions, presented as paintings were shown to focus groups.

4. Pilot Study

I ran a pilot study comprising three focus groups in order to analyse which methods from qualitative methodology were the most appropriate. The groups were made up of level 2 Fine Art students and staff from the University of Portsmouth and football supporters from Portsmouth Football Club.

Analysis of the pilot study led to a further nine focus groups including:

- Expert Readers; art critics/historians/painters
- Football stadium (Fratton Park Portsmouth) employees/ security guards
- Football supporters
- Staff and students from the University of Portsmouth.

Extracts from transcripts made from digital video recordings of the group discussions, were used to demonstrate the use of thematic and content analysis from qualitative methodology. Substantive statements made by participants, are used to evidence the identification of protagonists and Wollheim's term 'centrally imagining'.

Conclusions made from this analysis contribute to the discourse concerned with Wollheim's propositions concerning 'adequately informed' spectators in relation to representational painting.

5. Conclusions

Primary source observation and participation allowed me to gain a sense of aspects other than purely visual ones, which, as a painter and researcher, I believe is essential in order to communicate through the practice of representational painting. During the process my role changed. I became more culturally integrated and this allowed me to have a better grasp of what is at stake in 'informedness' within a particular cultural situation.

Three stages of my involvement can be highlighted through the paintings; observation, participant observation and informed artist. The narrative of the paintings moves from detachment as an observer, through 'native understanding' as a participant observer, to informed artist, as I became more involved with the participants of Portsmouth Football Club.

Analysis suggests that the paintings I produced as an informed artist (such as the painting of the stewards) allowed spectators greater access to the content of the image field more than those I produced during the beginning of my involvement as an observer.

Representational paintings made through this methodology can embody knowledge and this knowledge is established through a consensus between an informed painter and informed spectators who participate in the same image field. The resultant paintings could be used as examples for research in other image fields/cultural sites, offering collaborative possibilities between representational painting and other fields such as sociology and psychology.

Generally, it was a combination of the painterliness, technique, composition and painter's interpretation of the image field that made the images compelling for participants in the focus groups.

Important considerations for a practice led research project such as this are ethics, the production of diaries/journals and the transcripts from focus groups discussions.

There is substantial empirical material which establishes a body of knowledge found in the journals which document my observations, thoughts and reflections made during my participation at home matches at Fratton Park, PFC. These document my intentions, which are evidenced in the paintings made. By becoming a participant and observer within this particular culture the journals and the paintings made embody knowledge.

6. Future Research

The transcripts from the focus group discussions also evidence substantial empirical material, which contributes new knowledge concerned with how diverse audiences relate to representational paintings. Data analysed from focus group discussions contributes to a better understanding of the relationship between the intentions of a representational painter and differently informed spectators interpretations of paintings made within the image field of football culture. Analysis reveals that generally the spectators that participated in this project, referring to the painter and painting, mentioned matter, skill and labour and they referred to social and historical aspects of the image field. This suggests further research questions could focus on how audiences respond to other image fields/cultural sites such as homelessness, or comparisons between reception of different image fields such as football, rugby and opera.

Themes for the painter to focus on could be painterly processes and methods to portray aspects concerned with cultural identity, gender, crowd dynamics and body language within these fields.

The transcripts contain other themes that may be of interest to other researchers such as the relationship between representational painting, realism and photography.

Other questions concerning the impact a title has on the interpretation of a representational painting could be explored. When I ran the focus groups I did not provide titles for the paintings, however some groups discussed titles. Analysis suggests that representational paintings have the capacity to prompt memories for some spectators who 're-live' experiences without a painting having a title. How would a title affect the interpretation of such paintings? Would a title allow a spectator who has no knowledge of the image field access to the content of the painting? Due to the richness of the material embodied in the transcripts, I plan to post this research on a web site so that other interested parties can access it more readily.

Portsmouth City Museum invited me to exhibit the paintings as part of the 'Football in the City' exhibition. The museum would not insure the painting of the Southampton supporters placing it in a 'high risk' security category. The museum asked me if I would rather withdraw the painting from the exhibition. As this painting made up part of the research for this project it was important that it was exhibited alongside the other paintings. My feelings were that all responses to the paintings made up part of the research so to remove the painting would be interfering with the research process. The paintings were exhibited in the museum for six months and all paintings were returned in the condition in which I had lent them.

7. Outcomes

A significant outcome of this practice-led research project is that on 22/12/08 Portsmouth Football Club invited me to become Artist in Residence at the Club. This is the first time there has been such a position at the club. They would like me to continue to make paintings based on my observations and involvement with the club and exhibit the paintings at the club so that fans and workers alike may have access to them. This outcome is extremely important to me because it validates the importance of linking painterly realism and local cultural commitment of the kind supported by a nineteenth century painter such as Courbet, but less often found in the globalised art worlds of the twenty-first century. The paintings will be housed where they should be, at the heart of the community that they are concerned with.

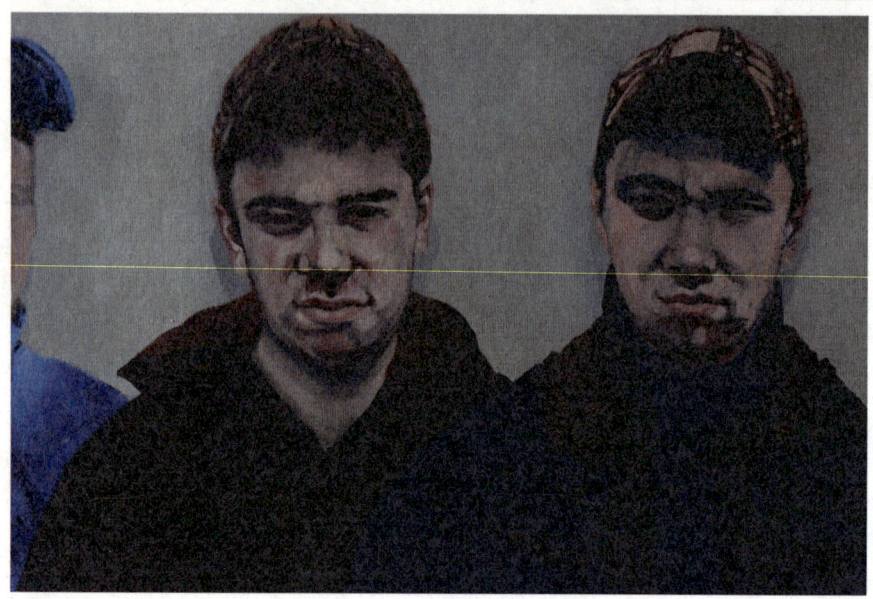

Figure 1: Jackie West (2004) *Pompey Boys*

Figure 2: Jackie West (2004) *Boots*

Figure 3: Jackie West (2007) *Portsmouth v Watford 18/11/06*

Figure 4: Jackie West (2007) *Portsmouth v Fulham 11/11/06*

Figure 5: Jackie West (2007) *Portsmouth v Southampton 24/04/05*

Notes

[1] The image field is the primary source observation area, which, for this project, is Fratton Park, Portsmouth Football Club's home ground.
[2] Richard Wollheim, *Painting as an Art* (London: Thames and Hudson, 1987).
[3] Timothy James Clark, *Image of the People* (London: Thames and Hudson, 1973).
[4] Ibid.
[5] This project initially involved taking part solely as an observer, but as my research has progressed and the results have been displayed or exhibited, I have become more of a 'participant observer', culminating in my becoming Artist in Residence at Portsmouth Football Club in December 2008. This gradual development of a more culturally integrated position has allowed me to have a better grasp of what is at stake in 'informedness' within a particular cultural situation.

Bibliography

Clark, Timothy James. *Image of the People*. London: Thames and Hudson, 1973.

Wollheim, Richard. *Painting as an Art*. London: Thames and Hudson, 1987.

Notes on Contributors

Jacek Burski is a PhD student in Sociology University of Łódz, Department of Sociology of Culture.

Paul Clark is a Lecturer in Journalism and Programme leader Sports Journalism in the University of Chester. He has industry experience; having previously worked as a sports reporter for a London-based news agency.

Carrie Dunn is about to submit her PhD in the experience of female football fans at Sheffield Hallam University. She is a journalist and also teaches as a guest lecturer around the UK.

Philip Grundon is an independent researcher who obtained a BA in Applied Digital Media from the University of Hull.

David Hindley is a member of the Sport and Leisure subject strand, helping to lead and deliver a number of modules. A recipient of a Jao Havalange Scholarship, David is undertaking research on behalf of the world's governing body for football, FIFA on social capital and volunteering in football.

Deirdre Hynes is Principal Lecturer at Manchester Metropolitan University. She is a relative newcomer to football research having previously studied gender, technological domestication and everyday life. Her current research focuses on female football fans and issues surrounding disenfranchisement, exclusion and empowerment. She is a passionate Liverpool fan and regular match-goer.

Katharine Jones is an Associate Professor of Sociology and Gender Studies at Philadelphia University. This paper is part of a larger book-length project about the changing nature of football fandom in England.

Annabel Kiernan is a Principal Lecturer at Manchester Metropolitan University. Her teaching and research interests focus on communuty engagement, Big Society, and UK public service reform. She is a season ticket holder and co-owner of FC United of Manchester since 2005.

Roy Krøvel is Associate Professor at Oslo and Akershus University College, Norway. He holds a PhD in history. His dissertation was on the relationship between the media and guerrilla organisations and indigenous peoples in Mexico and Central America. He currently teaches journalism.

Lucía Payero López is a member of the Department of Basic Legal Science in the University of Oviedo, Spain, in the area of Philosophy of Law.

Mick McKeown is a Principal Lecturer work in the School of Health at the University of Central Lancashire.

Darren Mundy is a Senior Lecturer in Digital Media in the School of Arts and New Media at the University of Hull.

Chris Porter is a Lecturer in Manchester Metropolitan University. His key research interests for include football fandom and politics, consumption, popular culture, class consciousness, globalisation and local identity. His doctoral thesis involved an exploration of the potential for political engagement within the football supporter culture of Manchester.

Alastair Roy is a Senior Lecturer in the School of Social Work at the University of Central Lancashire. His recent work has centred on substance use and misuse, the relationship between the socially engaged arts and wellbeing, and the role of cultural activity in health, welfare and justice.

Helen Spandler is a Senior Research Fellow in the School of Social Work at the University of Central Lancashire and also an associate of the Psychosocial Research Unit (PRU). Her main research area is mental health and critical social theory. She is research active in Football, gender and mental health.

Kate Themen is a Lecturer in Manchester Metropolitan University. She applies grounded research methodologies and an auto-ethnographic approach to her research in the fields of sport in social policy, sociology of football, aesthetics & gender and participation. She is a Manchester City fan for longer than she cares to remember!

Jackie West is a Lecturer in Animation and Course Leader of BA Animation in the University of Portsmouth. Her background is as an artist and she teaches drawing for animation. Her research interests are on relating interpretation of paintings with the intention of the artist.

Wojciech Woźniak is a Sociologist working in the Department of General Sociology, University of Łódź, Poland. Apart from sociology of sport, his fields of research interest include: social inequalities, political economy and sociology, and critical discourse analysis.

Index